THAT'S ONLY THE DOWN PAYMENT!

A Survival Manual for the Father of the Bride

MICHAEL M. WARREN, M.D.

Mike Klaur 1995

To Debora and Bruce
May you only have **sons**

NOTE WELL: I strongly advise you to hide this book. It contains very sensitive and secret material designed to help you survive your daughter's wedding. If it falls into the hands of the enemy, and they learn the material contained within, you will not only risk the usual hazards to success but add the additional hazard of your opponents learning about your intended tactics.

Contents

INTRODUCTION

Last weekend your daughter announced her engagement. I know, this is your dearest child. This is your little girl. This is the baby you held in one hand and now look at her. She is a grown woman, just about ready to acknowledge that you are not so dumb after all, and look at what she goes and does.

This past week things have gone crazy around your house. Your wife has already been to the emergency room twice to have the telephone removed from her ear. Everyone seems to know about the good news, and everyone has very strong opinions about what to do about the impending wedding.

There is talk about a wedding consultant, a wedding reception that will require the renting of Yankee Stadium, or the Astrodome if it looks like rain. All you can see are dollar signs passing in front of your eyes.

Then you remember some of the weddings you have attended recently. You remember the obvious opulence your friends have demonstrated with truckloads of flowers, twenty piece bands, gourmet dinners and new outfits for everyone from the mother of the bride to the flower girl.

Do you remember how the father of the bride looked during the festivities? Do you remember how you were so cute in the remarks you made about the cost of it all? Do you also remember how you smugly said that would never happen to you? Are you still smug? Then you are really in trouble.

You are about to enter one of the most difficult periods of your life. You only thought it was tough up to now. All those tricky business deals have been nothing compared to the negotiations you are about to enter. Dealing with your daughter as a teenager was a piece of cake compared to wedding plans. It's not just your daughter that will be a problem. In fact, she may be the least of your problems. Remember, your wife has been secretly yearning for this day ever since the delivery. She and her allies will carefully and thoroughly plan to demolish you financially, physically and psychologically.

1

Let's get one thing straight. I know you really do want to have a nice wedding for your daughter. You certainly don't want her to feel that she didn't have all the benefits that her friends had. She should have an occasion to look back on, with good feelings. The real question is the degree of the feelings. How much opulence is really necessary? There are all degrees and unless you are very strange, your concept of lavish and extravagant probably will not agree with the enemy.

What can you do about this? Well, all is not lost. You do have some options. First, stay calm. Losing your cool will only add to the general commotion and not get the job done.

Make sure you read this book. I strongly advise you to read it first, from cover to cover. Then keep it handy as a reference tool, since the wedding process probably will encompass several months and your needs for the material contained herein will vary. There will be times when you will need it constantly and other times when you might not need it for an hour or so.

Next, make sure you stay calm. Have I mentioned this before? Well, it bears restating. As the old saying goes, if you can stay calm when everyone else is going crazy then you obviously don't understand the severity of the situation. It's a good idea to make the enemy think you don't understand.

Plan a defense. Do not just play it by ear, one day at a time or from one crisis to another. Just like football, you need a game plan to be successful.

And one last thing—STAY CALM!!

Perhaps I should include a note about why I wrote this book. My oldest daughter recently became engaged and then married. I have just gone through the process (read that war). Since I never believed "misery likes company," I thought that sharing my newly acquired expertise might save you a bit of anxiety and help you get through your difficult time. Besides, if I sell enough of these books, I can help pay for the wedding.

This manual is meant to provide some helpful hints about what lies ahead for you now that a wedding is in your future. It is not meant to be complete. It would take volumes to include all possibilities and when that was done, something would still be left out. Some stories are highly individualistic, personal and not for widespread dissemination.

Rather, I want to give you the flavor of what is in store for you, to whet your appetite. There is no question that you are about to get involved in a project with considerable associated expense. This book is intended to minimize your expense, not eliminate it.

I have attempted to maintain a light atmosphere throughout this book. Even though some of my comments might be considered humorous, they are not meant to be inconsequential. This is a serious subject, but if presented too seriously will only result in further depression. Do not minimize the problem, but do not begin mourning either. Keep a steady and true course and you will reach your destination. You will be a happy but broke father of the bride.

Following each section, where appropriate, I have included check lists for your convenience. Be sure to follow these guidelines, or at least remember "I told you so!"

I would be remiss if I did not acknowledge the support I received from two individuals. Dr. Catherine Moore read and advised me on the style and grammar of the text. Mr. Claude Allen is the brilliant illustrator whose work has immeasurably enhanced the text. I could not have done this without them.

THE ENEMY

As in any battle or war it is essential to know your enemy, not only to know who they are but to learn as much as possible about their habits, idiosyncrasies, strengths and weaknesses. Only then can you exploit them appropriately for victory.

Here is where you have the edge: you've been living with most of the enemy for years. You, of all people, should know and understand all their moves. You know all about their spending habits, where they shop, the kind of things they like and how much money they spend. You have been paying their bills for a long time.

Knowing about these people is important, but doing something about them is much more important. Why haven't you been doing something all along? Well, I guess it wasn't so important before but, as you will see, it now becomes essential.

Let's look at some of the enemy individually. They fall into two main categories. First are the members of your family, both your immediate family and your new family, acquired for you by your daughter when she fell in love with your future son-in-law.

Then there are the groups of friends, relatives and strangers called vendors. You will need to become educated about all of the enemy in order to have any chance (remote as it is) of success in this wedding war.

The Bride

We have to talk about the bride. This is particularly painful since this bride is also your daughter. Remember, she is your little girl. She is the one you dote over most. She is probably the oldest. The one whose photo you took every minute when she was a kid. The only one you took pictures of every day, in all positions, doing all sorts of cute things. (By the time the other kids came along the novelty was gone and they were hardly remembered.)

Forget all that. She is still the enemy. Although she may not be the chief culprit, (we'll get to her in a minute), she does represent a major threat for the next several months. I know you brought her up right, you taught her thrift and economy. When you did, she wasn't in love: now the game has changed. Don't expect her to apply logic or make any sense until after the honeymoon. Once again, she is in love.

I would strongly advise you to treat her kindly and carefully. Don't expect her to make decisions quickly or easily, and above all don't expect her to remember previous decisions. You can bank on the fact that she will change her mind almost daily if not more often. There is no advantage in reminding her of previous decisions she made. And don't bother pointing out now that since she has made a new decision you expect her to remember it and keep it. She is in love.

In my war, I thought it would be good strategy to write decisions down in a book, once they were made. It made no difference. Lengthy discussions, logically derived plans, carefully documented decisions all changed with the weather. Remember, she is in love, or have I mentioned that before?

Anyway, she is your little girl and you did love her, and even now feel a kind of affection for her. Remember, there is life after the wedding. Some day you will need her, at least in your old age. You better play your cards close to the vest. Stay on her good side, if for no other reason then for compassion for your fellow human beings, particularly the groom. One day the groom will become the husband. He will need all the help he can get, and regardless of what you think of the twerp that stole your baby, give him a break. He is still a fellow male. Even though you are not sure about that, I'll bet your daughter can tell you. But that may be a question you don't want to ask her just now.

Finally, remember, she is in love.

The Mother of the Bride

Now, we have to talk about the real problem. That's right, the mother of the bride. I know that you have been to several weddings, even though you may never have had a vested interest. You do know that the mother of the bride is traditionally escorted down the aisle by an usher, before the ceremony starts. She sits quietly, perhaps tearfully, but with no real part in the ceremony. After all, you will give the bride away. The happy couple will be the center of attention. Even the cute little ring bearer will get more attention than the mother of the bride.

So how come she is generally considered the biggest threat in this war they call a wedding? How come a quiet, unassuming person who always remains in the background becomes a ferocious monster bent on destroying you financially, mentally and physically in only a few short months? And what, do you suppose, is the physiologic stimulus that causes this Jekyll and Hyde condition in a person who otherwise spent only half your income on her own clothes, jewelry and perfumes?

I will tell you frankly that I don't know. But it does happen, just as sure as the swallows return to Capistrano and the lemmings find their way to the sea. Your wife is no different. About all you can say in her behalf is that it is a reaction probably beyond her control, so that you can't really hold her responsible. Nevertheless, if you don't take certain actions you are going to be in big trouble. I just hope you purchased this survival manual long enough before the wedding to do some good. Actually, you needed this to read on your honeymoon, because some long term strategies I will discuss later do take some planning. In fact, some men not only need this manual during the honeymoon, but even well before that.

Back to your wife. She is the main enemy, and if you don't think so now, you will soon. You have to treat her like the enemy. Do not shoot her. That's not what I mean. Consider yourself part of the CIA and be clandestine. Gather intelligence, and other information, without tipping your hand. Don't let her think you are even remotely interested. She will try to get you to participate in the decision making, but don't fall for that old trick. If the decision turns out to be the correct one, she will take credit for it. If it was incorrect guess who is going to get blamed for being stupid? More stupid than usual, that is.

Involving you in the plans seems to be a goal of the entire enemy

group. Don't let it happen. This is extremely important advice and very difficult to follow. Your patience will be sorely tried and you will witness countless hours of enemy discussions about a given topic with a final solution that will be blatantly inappropriate. Your natural tendency, as the clever and astute individual that you are, is to jump in and try to set them straight. Let me repeat—DON'T DO IT!

What should you do about all the good ideas you do have? Once again, you have to be clever. Try to find some way that the enemy thinks of the ideas by themselves. You do remember when your daughter, the very same daughter who is about to leave the nest, would never even look at any boy you suggested might be a good date for her? It didn't matter that he was a Cornell University graduate and a medical student whose parents were multimillionaires, or that he made Robert Redford look like Quasimoto. If you suggested him, he had to be a "dog." Remember how you had to engineer a chance meeting or a recommendation from someone in her own peer group? Well, that's what you have to do with the enemy in this situation.

Try leaving some notes, or perhaps a brochure or a photo of some event that will suggest the idea to them. And never, never try to take credit when they tell you about their great new idea. In fact, don't try to take credit, even years later. It will do no good. Nevertheless, if they do "think of it by themselves" and it is the correct idea, be happy.

Even though I told you not to try to give advice outright, do listen. Pay close attention. You will not only learn about the enemy, but you also may stay out of trouble later. On the other hand, even though you have to pay close attention, don't look like you are paying attention at all. Try to learn how to look like you are asleep, or engrossed in a book, while you are listening. If you can perfect this ploy, it may stand you in good stead as a lifelong tool, getting you out of all sorts of future problems.

From this very moment until after all the plans have been completed, all the bills paid and everyone has recovered, you will have to be constantly on your guard when dealing with your wife. If you display any tendency toward being contrary, she will undertake the chore of outwitting you in order to get her way. Be prepared at all times for her attack. She may be particularly adept at waking you up in the middle of the night to extract an agreement about some need for more money. I would strongly advise not sleeping at all when she is around. Consider her as John Wayne considered the Apache. If you must sleep, do it with one eye open.

Also watch out for places like the theater, breakfast, and the bathroom, all well known ambush spots. And remember, she has the ability to subcontract the work out to others in the ranks of the enemy, particularly the grandmother of the bride—that's your mother, dummy. You do remember her methods? If not, talk to your father immediately.

The Grandmother of the Bride

We need to talk a little about the grandmother of the bride. Try to remember that, in all probability, she had very little to do with the planning of your wedding. Yet, like all women, she was genetically and environmentally prepared to be intimately involved. What that means is she probably is frustrated that she had nothing to do with your wedding, and eager to participate in your daughter's.

Worse, your daughter and wife probably will love to have her involved. After all, your daughter's experience in spending has only existed for a few years. Your wife has had some additional experience, but nothing like your mother's. Now there is a really experienced spender. Years of training have paid off. Watch her. See how she can detect the most expensive store in a shopping mall, and the most expensive clothes in the store. Notice how she completely ignores the price tag, or the sale items. She is an expert at comparative shopping to get just the right color, accessory or size, but never price. Are you getting the idea?

Not only that, you may be able to intimidate your daughter some and your wife a little, but your mother—never. No chance you can scare her with any of the usual ploys. After all, you can't cut off her allowance or limit her budget. If you stay out all night with the boys, she doesn't care. And, you will have trouble even bribing her. Remember, she's your mother.

The Sisters of the Bride

If you really planned poorly, there probably will be other females around the house. Siblings of the bride, your other daughters, will rapidly join the ranks of the enemy. After all, why should they be different from the others? They do not want to be left out in the cold. This is too good an opportunity for them to miss. And besides, they need the training. Your first experience as father of the bride probably will be the easiest one for you. Your enemy probably will have some compassion for your misery the first time. After they go through the process and see what they could have and should have done, you won't stand a chance during future wedding wars. Your other daughters understand this concept and want you to make all the mistakes for this wedding, so their's can be "perfect."

They will be watching and waiting for the right time to pounce and put in their two cents. Be careful. By the way, how many daughters do you have, lucky? You better pay close attention to the section of this manual devoted to long range planning, to see what you should have done.

The Mother of the Groom

Let me add a few words about another enemy that is closely involved in the process. We must not forget the mother of the groom. Have you met her yet? You do know she is closest personal friends with the entire city. Her address book is larger than the telephone book, since it contains those unlisted numbers as well. Also, she has been invited to all the weddings that have taken place in your town in the past twenty years and she does "owe" those people something. She has already told them about the wedding. She has obligated you to invite them all.

But she is a smart lady and knows that it would be an unfair financial burden on you to ask you to pay for all her friends, especially when you hardly know them. She or her husband may make you an offer to help pay for the wedding. Just try it buster! Do you expect your wife to have to spend the rest of her life feeling like a second class citizen, embarrassed that she couldn't afford to pay for her own daughters wedding? Not on your life. She would rather have you go into debt (which you probably will do anyway), than have everyone in town know that you didn't pay for it all. You can certainly do without a few luxuries for a few years. And I do mean you, not her.

CHECK LIST
The Enemy

❏ Identify the enemy
❏ Identify all enemy
❏ Identify their strengths
❏ Identify their weaknesses
❏ Identify their idiosyncrasies
❏ Identify their spending habits
❏ Pay attention to enemy discussions
❏ Don't give advice or opinions
❏ Don't make decisions
❏ Get enemy to adopt your ideas without letting them know
❏ Watch out for sneak attacks
❏ Try intimidation only if all else fails

Anti Enemy Strategies

So much for the immediate enemy. Before we discuss the rest of the enemy, I want to suggest some tactics to deal with these people.

First of all, the best you can hope for is to cut your losses. You cannot win. Maintain the best front you can. Any good general knows the best defense is a good offense. But like any good football coach knows, a good defense wins ball games. Give me Bear Bryant anytime.

It's a good idea if all of these immediate family enemies live in different cities. With any luck, your daughter will be working in a city at least 500 miles away. Since she met her fiance while working, there is a good chance that his mother will live closer to him than to you.

Perhaps your younger daughters will be away at school. If you can keep them all apart your biggest expense may be the telephone bill. But if you let them get together and thereby give them unlimited time to plan, you will be at significantly greater risk. Work on it! Perhaps you will be lucky enough to have this wedding during a recession, when prices are down and when everybody is trying to underbid the competition for your business. That's another good strategy, if you can work it. Of course, the risk you run is that the great bargains will allow the enemy to increase their desires. Oh well, try the lottery.

CHECK LIST
Anti Enemy Strategies

❑   Be prepared to lose
❑   Cut your loses
❑   Make sure your enemies all live in different cities
❑   Have the wedding during a recession
❑   Move out
❑   Don't let your wife intimidate you

Vendors

We will discuss individual vendors and the problems associated with them when we discuss the strategies you need to develop to deal with the myriad of details of the wedding proper. But a few words about vendors, as a group, are in order.

Sometime during the ordeal of planning, you may get the impression that there is a conspiracy among all of these people, directed entirely against you. Do not feel paranoid. You are correct, they are against you. Remember, even paranoid people can be persecuted.

And, remember, it's not just the money. These people earn plenty of money. I mean, there are only three things in life that are sure, weddings, divorces and death. (I hear we may not have taxes soon.) So they will have lots of income. They do it for the sport. The more you squirm, the better they like it.

The vendors are in the business of selling weddings. The more, the better and the more lavish, better yet. You can expect a variety of tactics to be employed by most of them.

Watch out for the "you wouldn't want the bride to feel second class, would you?" ploy. Playing on your sympathies is standard procedure. "Oh, you could settle for this plain old inexpensive dress, but just take a look at this modern and very popular model." "This is the latest thing this year." "You wouldn't want to drive last years model, would you?" It goes on and on.

Beware of "the chain is as strong as the weakest link" story. If you buy the best dress, rent the nicest reception hall, and serve the best food, you wouldn't want to serve cheap liquor or wine. That theory will get you every time. It's the first step that leads you down the road to financial ruin. That's why you have to watch every plan, every purchase, every contract with every vendor. Anyone can start the snowball rolling down the hill and force you into bigger and bigger purchases.

The problem is, you cannot appear to be too interested, too picky or too cheap. You have to keep your distance and at the same time exert the proper influence so as not to relinquish the control to the enemy. It's really hard to give absolute advice on how to do this, since each of the enemy is a little bit different and will require different tactics. Just don't ignore the necessity of keeping on top of vendor negotiations even though you have to appear non controlling and acquiescent.

It might sound like a good idea to let the enemy deal with the vendors without you present and then for you to meet and deal with the vendors yourself at a later time. This might work, if you and the enemy were actually working together trying to get the best deal for the best price. If you were buying a car, for example, working independently, and appearing to put the salesman between the two of you has a lot of merit. This is the so called "good cop, bad cop" method. It works well if both "cops" act as a team, with the same goals. I'm not sure you and your wife have the same goals in this project.

The bottom line is you better be prepared to get educated about vendors and how to deal with them, when you are the only one interested in financial considerations. Also, you will find vendors selling things you never realized existed before and services you only dreamed about. Don't be surprised when you are faced with the questions of ice carvings, lace embroidery or anthurium. And remember that age old adage "caveat emptor" that translated from the latin means "let the buyer beware."

CHECK LIST
Vendors

- ❑ Dress cheaply
- ❑ Look poor
- ❑ Act uninterested
- ❑ Don't be intimidated
- ❑ Question their quality
- ❑ Question their ancestry
- ❑ Play one against the other
- ❑ Comparison shop
- ❑ Tell them you comparison shop
- ❑ Test what they sell
- ❑ Don't accept the first offer
- ❑ Bargain (negotiate)
- ❑ Tell them you refer good vendors to others
- ❑ Tell them you tell all your friends about poor vendors
- ❑ Don't fall for sympathy
- ❑ Don't believe they are losing money on you
- ❑ Don't fall for emotional sales tactics
- ❑ Always sit in a corner of their store with your back to the wall
- ❑ Read the contract several times—including the fine print
- ❑ Ask questions
- ❑ Don't let your wife intimidate you

Advisors

Your family will have a variety of advisors available to help you with the plans for this wedding. In fact, although I will describe several to you, please remember that EVERYONE is an advisor. After all, can you possibly think of any other area in which more people have had experience? Although experience does not equal expert, you can't tell them that. Not only is everyone an advisor, but everyone will gladly give you advice, in great detail and often conflicting.

Let's look as some of the types of people who will be your advisors. First are the professional advisors, the wedding directors or consultants. These people are usually very experienced in making wedding plans and even more experienced in charging for their services. You can be assured of their expertise because the enemy would not deal with anyone but the best. You can be assured of their charging because you will get the bill. We will discuss them in more detail in the individual strategy section.

Wedding directors and individual vendors are experts in their area; amateur advisors include everyone else. Amateur advisors will include both family and friends. They know everything. They will tell you everything. Usually they won't even wait for you to ask, but will volunteer the information spontaneously. They will expect you to follow their advice to the letter and, if you should be so ungrateful not to follow it, they will usually become angry with you for your stupidity. After all, they know they are correct and you also should recognize their expertise.

Sometimes you can work this to your advantage. If you adopt the attitude that their advice is worthless, and share with them your opinion, you may get them so angry that they will refuse to attend the wedding. Of course, that means you won't have their sparkling wit and personality at your affair and you certainly can't expect them to send a gift, but you won't have to pay for them either. Only you know what the long term implications of such an action may mean to you and your family. The decision will have to be yours and may vary from person to person. If you choose wisely, this may be the chance you have been waiting for and trim your address book of those unwanted people.

Unfortunately, this strategy usually works better for acquaintances than for family. You will be successful in insulting and distancing your family, but you will not be successful in eliminating them. You may have to put up with them, anyway, but also will have to put up with their continued anger and insults. It's your decision.

A less drastic strategy is better. Perhaps you need to learn how to listen to these people, present a pleasant smile and assure them that you will give their advice every consideration. Do not forget to mention that it is really your wife and daughter who are planning the event and direct them to discuss the issue with the decision makers. Of course, if the advice is what you were going to do anyway, then use it to your advantage. Thank them profusely for their opinion, tell them how valuable it is and assure them that you intend to follow it to the letter. Then, make sure you don't let them find out your ploy.

CHECK LIST
Advisors

❑ Try not to bring up the subject of the wedding
❑ Listen politely
❑ Ask for proof of their statements
❑ Nod "yes" a lot
❑ Question their experience
❑ Question their ancestry
❑ Ignore their advice
❑ Watch out for professional advisors
❑ Watch out for amateur advisors
❑ Get a second opinion
❑ Promise you will do it only if you were going to do it anyway
❑ Blame all decisions on the enemy
❑ Don't let your wife intimidate you

More Anti Enemy Strategies

There are a few more general strategies that you can use to defeat the enemy. First, remember the "divide and conquer" strategy. If you can find ways to get your wife, daughter and other enemy to disagree on any or all issues, or even better, if you can get them actually to have a knock-down, drag-out fight about it, you have a chance to come on as the "knight in shining armor" and save they day. Make sure that when you do save the day, you do it with the best (read that cheapest) solution to the problem.

I don't think it pays to try to have all the enemy make up after the fight. They may then go right back to attacking you. If you keep them at odds, it may help you with the next decision. There are some long term implications to this strategy that you may want to consider. There will be a life after the wedding and you will have to maintain some degree of relationship with these people, this strategy should be used sparingly.

Another ploy is to get sick. This can get complicated, but there are a variety of ways you can make illness work to your benefit. You can just get mildly ill, but ill enough to avoid dealing with the decisions that have to be made. Alternatively, you could get seriously ill. So ill, if you want to carry it to extremes, that the wedding would be called off. Or at least ill enough so you could participate if it was just a "small and intimate" affair without throngs of people.

If you do use this strategy, I would advise that you choose your illness carefully. Try to find one that doesn't lead to long term consequences. Try to avoid a heart attack. You may achieve your immediate goal but the long term problems with everyone treating you like an invalid (including your wife in dealing with your sexual habits) may not be what you want.

Perhaps some fainting spells, particularly stress related are appropriate. After all, you wouldn't want to be walking down the aisle and faint in front of all those people. Wouldn't it be better just to have a small gathering of immediate family? Then, of course, you wouldn't have to faint any more later.

Finally, how about a timely fire, or flood for that matter? It reminds me of the story of the two retired businessmen from New York, Sam and Max, who met each other on the beach in Florida. Sam asked his friend Max how he was doing and what was happening in his business. Max told him that he was retired because after the fire and the

insurance paid the claim, he didn't feel much like starting over. Max then asked Sam how his business was doing. Sam replied that he had a similar instance with a flood, and after the insurance claim was paid he didn't feel much like starting over either. At that point, Max said; "Flood! How do you have a flood?"

I really can't give you any advice about how to have a fire or flood, mainly because I prefer to stay out of jail. You'll have to work that out for yourself.

CHECK LIST
More Anti Enemy Strategies

❏   Keep enemy arguing with each other—divide and conquer
❏   Get sick
❏   Have a fire or flood
❏   Don't let your wife intimidate you

THE (so called) ALLIES

Are you ready for some good news? You are not totally alone in this battle. You may have some allies. We need to discuss them, but before we do, you always need to remember the craftiness of your opponents. Someone who may be your ally today may not be tomorrow. It takes a strong commitment. Do they have what it takes?

Remember communism and the so called "fifth column" of spies that were planted throughout the free world in order to give information to the enemy. I doubt many of you remember World War II and the concern that even patriots could give valuable information to the enemy without realizing what they were doing. The posters said "Loose Lips Sink Ships." They meant just that. Seemingly valueless information could be gathered by the enemy and pieced together into intelligence information about our plans and troop movements.

Remember, please, that even your potential allies may need to be observed closely and continuously to ensure their allegiance. And, even if you are sure of their support, also be sure they are not divulging important strategies, inadvertently, to the enemy.

The Father Of The Groom

You envy him. I do, too. But before you become too jealous, please remember that the father of the groom has some problems himself. Tradition dictates that he is responsible for the planning and expenses of the rehearsal dinner.

Rehearsal dinners have changed a bit during the past few years. No longer does the wedding party simply go to the church or synagogue, practice the ceremony and then go out for a bite to eat. Moreover, the dinner often includes all the out of town guests that may number several hundred, and also may include a band and be more lavish then the wedding itself.

Accordingly, you might want to share this book with the father of the groom. Better yet, make him buy his own. We will discuss rehearsal dinners in the next section; nevertheless, the father of the groom can be a very important ally in your struggle. He should have the ear of the mother of the groom and perhaps can influence her to influence the mother of the bride. Even if this is not possible, both the father and mother of the groom will have to make out a guest list and he can influence the length of that list.

A word of caution is in order: as I already mentioned, the father of the groom has the ear of the mother of the groom. He may be even closer than that. Even if he is not, he spends much more time with the mother of the groom than you do and he may inadvertently leak your strategies. Be careful.

The Grandfather Of The Bride

If you have trouble with all of these titles, the grandfather of the bride is your father. Can you trust the old man? You have to answer that, I can't. A great deal depends on the rest of your siblings. Do you have sisters? Was he involved with their weddings as you are with your daughter's? If he was then you have a chance. At least he can give you moral support.

Wait a minute! He isn't the type of grandfather that loves to give your kids gifts and otherwise spoil them, is he? If he is, maybe you should switch him over to the enemy list, and fast.

The Brothers Of The Bride

Well, I guess we're down to the bottom of the list. All you have left are the brothers of the bride—your sons. Oh boy, are you in trouble. Did you ever think you would have to rely on them? With any luck, your daughter is an only child.

THE GROOM:

REMEMBER, HE'S iN LOVE!

THE NEUTRALS

The Groom

There is only one neutral, the groom. Remember, he is in love. It really isn't fair to expect too much from him. Besides, he's got his own problems. He will try to please his bride. For that matter, he will try to please everyone, but in priority order. I hope you know where you are on the priority list. Please don't try to pull any power plays on him, I really feel sorry for the guy. Besides, I do believe that he is the only male child for two generations on his side of the family. You should buy him a copy of this book and give it to him when he becomes at risk for fathering a daughter. I guess that's immediately.

CHECK LIST
The Allies and Neutrals

- ☐ Watch out for spies
- ☐ Watch out for "loose lips"
- ☐ Watch out for the grandfather of the bride. He may be an enemy. He loves his granddaughter
- ☐ The brothers of the bride are probably worthless. Don't count on them
- ☐ Don't count on the groom. He is in love
- ☐ Assume you have no allies—act accordingly
- ☐ Don't let your wife intimidate you

STRATEGIES—LONG TERM

If you had the luxury of time, you could have planned future events with foresight to achieve your goals. I'm sure that is your usual practice. Your current predicament was probably just a temporary lapse in thinking. The problem is time flies when you're having fun, and I mean that literally. Here are a few strategies you could have used if you would have planned ahead.

Family Planning

When I talk about long range planning, I really mean long range planning. Perhaps that is why giving a copy of this book to the groom may even be a little bit too late. This section pertains to those men, or perhaps boys, who have yet to declare their marital intentions. Hopefully, they don't even have marital intentions.

There are certain facts they should learn about the intended bride's habits that can be of critical importance. If you had considered them, you wouldn't be in this fix now. Can she sew? Does she like to sew? Does she like to sew wedding dresses? Does her skin break out in an allergic reaction to silver and gold? Can she balance a check book? Does she hate lace and pearls? Do *you* get the idea????

Sex Selection

Obviously, if having children was so important back then, you should have had only male offspring. At least your financial burden would have been considerably less. After all, even if you had to bail your sons out of jail several times, it still would not have exceeded the cost of even a small wedding.

Without going into a lengthy lecture on genetics, it really is all your fault, anyway. You see, the gene that determines sex is carried by you. Your wife, or any female for that matter, has two "X" chromosomes. You have one "X" and one "Y." It's the "Y" chromosome that is required to have a male offspring. Therefore, you actually determine whether your child will be a boy or girl.

Now your only problem is to make sure a sperm with a "Y" chromosome fertilizes your wife's egg. Good luck! Ask any woman, especially a grandmother, and she will give you at least one foolproof method to ensure your children's sex can be selected. Sometimes the methods require extensive maneuvering, and sometimes downright acrobatics.

I must admit that I don't hold much faith in those "old wive's tales" but you really haven't got much choice about selecting the sex of your children unless you try them. Or, you can revert to what some might consider drastic. There are some cultures where sons are important and daughters of not much value so that newborn female children are routinely drowned.

Come to think of it, I'm really not sure whether they drown newborn female children or cats. Oh well, either way it is a drastic measure. We'll see how you feel about it as the wedding date gets closer.

Brainwashing

Another technique that may seem drastic, but not in comparison to drowning, is to develop a long term system of brainwashing. There are a variety of ways to do this. For example, you could visit with your daughter daily (not a bad practice anyway) and constantly remind her to have a small, simple marriage. Some experts say the best time to do this is just as she is dozing off to sleep. I'm not sure, but I do know it has to be done daily and that you have to start at a very young age—say within a week of her birth. By the way, I don't think it's a good idea to tell your wife what you are doing. She probably won't appreciate your attempts, so keep it a "secret" between you and your little girl. I must admit this technique did not help me, but I don't think I left any lasting scars. I do worry that the attempts I made worked to the opposite of my intentions. It's one way to explain the wedding plans my wife and daughter arranged.

Brainwashing has to be on a long term basis and include much more than whispering in your daughter's ear. You have to take certain steps during her development to ensure success. For example, establish a good work ethic in your daughter, perhaps a part time job at age four, moving to full time employment by age eight or nine. Do not, under any circumstances, give her any money or money substitutes, like charge cards. Don't let her play monopoly or any other games that include play money. Teach her to hate boys. Encourage her to play football, hockey and prizefighting. Send her to an all girls school and above all, delay her dating as long as possible, say to about age forty.

Community Activities

Most men enjoy donating some of their free time to community activities. Some of us help with the United Way, some with our local historical society. In fact, there are a huge number of groups that would welcome volunteers. But have you considered your church or synagogue? These groups are often desperate for lay support in any number of ways. Consider joining such a group, devote your time, work hard and try to achieve the lofty status of membership on the governing board. Then you can start to influence the ceremonial rules and regulations.

For example, wouldn't it be good if your church or synagogue would adopt the policy that simple wedding ceremonies were the most meaningful for the participants and receptions should be limited to champagne (or punch—depending on church rules) and cake? If this became the institution policy then you wouldn't have to worry about keeping up with the Jones' and you could maintain the full spiritual meaning of the occasion. Increasing your religious activity can never hurt.

Business Moves

I don't know what you do for a living, but let me suggest how lucky you would be if you were in the catering business, or perhaps if you were a florist or even better if you sold wedding dresses. Just because you became a physician, lawyer, dentist, engineer or some other seemingly highly paid profession, you still will have a problem paying for this wedding. It's really too bad you didn't plan ahead. Of course, if you have other unmarried daughters, it's still not too late to start a new business.

These are just a few of the ideas that you could have considered if you had just planned ahead. More will come to you and you really should kick yourself for not doing a better job all those years ago. I don't understand why we men keep making the same mistake over and over again. I guess we never learn.

CHECK LIST
Strategies—Long Term

❑ Marry someone who:
    Loves to sew
    Hates jewelry
    Can balance a checkbook
    Hates satin, lace and pearls
❑ Only have sons
❑ Brainwash all female children
❑ Join church/synagogue board of directors and make rules against expensive weddings
❑ Buy or start a:
    food catering business
    florist shop
    wedding supply store
❑ Don't let your wife intimidate you

STRATEGIES—SHORT TERM

Well, here we are. I suspect you didn't have a chance to employ any of the long-term strategies we have already discussed. What you have to do now is cut your losses. You are going to have a wedding and you must try to ease the pain as much as possible. The good news is that you now can identify the enemy and allies. You know that the enemy is strong and your allies weak, if not nonexistent. What success you will have will be due to your own diligence and ingenuity.

The bad news is that there are a million ways to mess up and a huge number of details to keep in mind because each and every one can be a potential major loss of funds. You know your wife and daughter have a book with all the details of their game plan. Now you have one also.

Speaking of their book, try to find it. Read it privately, but thoroughly, so that you can learn their plans. Remember that old adage bridge players have used for centuries: "One peek is worth two finesses." This is not a time to worry about ethics or morals. If you can learn their plans you have gained a major advantage. Remember that their book will be continuously changed and updated. Keep your eyes open.

Since there are so many details to consider, it is best to discuss each of them individually and plan a strategy to deal with each of them. Even so, no list I can compile can be complete. New wedding traditions are constantly evolving and old ones often give way to new ones with rapidity. It's amazing how fast the wedding underground adopts new ideas and still convinces you and me of their long standing tradition that we must follow.

Elopement

We need to talk about elopement because it's always the first thing that comes to mind when the father of the bride learns about the impending wedding. It does sound clever. The problem is it almost never works. But we have all heard of cases where the loving couple did elope and "hope springs eternal." It's worth a try, but don't get depressed when all you get are a bunch of laughing, "Oh, dad"s, and some question about your own ancestry.

Calculate a fair price for what you think a wedding should cost. Then double that figure and offer it as an inducement to elope. It still will not cost as much as the wedding, but it may be enough to make them think. Be sure the enemy understands that you will not only pay a huge sum for the elopement itself, but you also will pay all the expenses for the honeymoon, and even a ladder. (I wonder if anyone uses a ladder anymore?)

Also remember that even though you get an initial turn down, the thought of elopement looks better and better to the enemy as the plans for the wedding become more and more complicated and tempers are strained.

It is a very old ploy. I believe there are even biblical references to its use. The enemy will be prepared for you and their response probably will be resounding. About the only chance it has to work is if the bride and the mother of the bride hate each other, or if they grow to hate each other over the wedding plans. Even then, their chance of engaging in their own truce is much greater than accepting your generous elopement offer.

CHECK LIST
Strategies—Short Term
and
Elopement

- ❑ Find and study the enemy wedding books, notes and other documents
- ❑ Offer elopement
- ❑ Make it an appealing offer
- ❑ Repeat the offer periodically
- ❑ Don't give up
- ❑ Provide the ladder
- ❑ Pay for the trip
- ❑ Talk to the groom "man to man"
- ❑ Leave travel brochures around
- ❑ Don't take credit if it works
- ❑ Don't let your wife intimidate you

Pre-nuptial Parties

The key word here is parties. Weddings mean parties. Any excuse will be good enough for a party. I have no idea where all the traditions came from that require these parties, but they are required. The good news is that you may not have much direct responsibility, either financial or planning, for these parties. Oh, they will cost you something. If nothing else, a new wardrobe will be required for you and your immediate family so that you can look acceptable to the rest of your family, friends and new in-laws. But the major expenses may be spared, if.....

Hope that someone else volunteers to have these parties, especially the engagement party. Try some of the bride's grandparents, friends or close family members. Try the in-laws. Try praying. Unfortunately, if nothing works, try the bank because you will find that you are the host for the engagement party.

Engagement Party

After all, the world does have to know that the happy couple is engaged to be married. No, a simple newspaper article, with photograph will not suffice. You need a small party to celebrate the good news. Actually, study the guest list carefully. It will give you an indication of the potential size of the wedding. Now, don't expect the list to be the same. There will be many more people invited to the wedding but if the engagement list is 400 to 500 guests, get ready.

If you do have to foot the bill for the engagement party, shoot for a casual affair, perhaps at home, perhaps a barbecue. Try to point out that if it costs too much, you won't have any money left for the wedding itself, but both of us know how far that argument is going to get you. If you're lucky, you should be able to avoid the need for a band, major floral arrangements and other expenses.

The tendency of the enemy will be to have a big party. Remember their underlying philosophy and the basic need for gifts. Engagement parties call for gifts. Not gifts for you, but gifts for the engaged couple. You will spend the money and they will get the gifts, but it really doesn't matter as you probably have all the stuff they are going to get, anyway. You should if your wife is at least like the average wife. It's just like the old story of the family income; all the money you earn is both of yours and all the money she earns is hers. Why do you pay tax on both? Oh, well, join the club.

Showers

Showers are another interesting tradition. I don't know how the tradition started. For that matter, I don't even know how they got their name, but showers have been around for a long time. There are many types and formats for these showers, and are usually "given" to the bride by friends and relatives. They traditionally involve only women, although that tradition is changing and more are becoming affairs for couples. Cucumber sandwiches are being replaced by large and elaborate buffet meals and the caterers are very happy.

Gifts are also involved with showers. Most brides are given several showers during the weeks before the wedding. Some of them will involve themes such as a lingerie shower or a crystal shower or any number of varieties where the category of gifts is specified.

The showers may be designed for different types of guests. One may be for the bride's friends of her age and given by one of them while another is for friends of the mother of the bride and so forth. Some guests may find themselves invited to several or even all of the showers. Each one will require a gift. I'm sure it will make you feel badly to see these people spending all that money for your daughter's showers, won't it? There may be some justice, but only a little.

I've never been to one of the showers designed for women only. I really don't know what goes on at these functions, except the few times I've peeked. I get the distinct impression that the major activity at a wedding shower is to have the guests brainstorm for more ways to spend your money on bigger and newer wedding plans.

Be that as it may, financing showers usually does not fall to the father of the bride so, with the exception of new clothes for your family to wear to these functions, you should be fairly safe. Remember, of course, that many of the same people will be at the same showers and you really can't expect your female family members to wear the same outfit to all of them.

Bachelor/Bachelorette Parties

Here's some more good news. (It may be the last.) Bachelor parties have been a tradition for a long time. I'm sure you remember yours, which was probably a sedate affair. A group of your friends met at someone's home, drank some fruit punch and reminisced about old times. I think today's parties are about the same. No matter; planning is usually done by the best man and even if you are invited, you should only have to pay your way. (By the way, if you are invited, I may have been right about the type of party, at least the first part, before you go home.)

Newer on the scene are bachelorette parties. Remember, women are liberated now and there is no question that the ladies have the same rights and desires that men have always enjoyed. Again, I'm not sure what goes on at a typical bachelorette party. I have tried to peek in and see what is happening, but at most of the nightclubs where these parties are held, there is some very large, muscular individual at the door who will not let me in. I do know that everyone usually has a good time, and nobody will talk about the activities. Bachelorette parties, at least, shouldn't cost you much.

CHECK LIST
Pre-nuptial Parties

- ❑ Avoid an engagement party
- ❑ If you can't avoid it, make it informal
- ❑ Serve only pretzels and peanuts
- ❑ Encourage as many showers as you can afford new clothes for
- ❑ Budget for clothes
- ❑ Make sure you don't sponsor a shower
- ❑ Don't go to the bachelor party
- ❑ If you do go, leave early. You won't miss anything
- ❑ Don't even think about going to the bachelorette party
- ❑ Don't let your wife intimidate you

The Budget

So much for any good news. The rest of our short term strategies will all be bad news, with some of them being terrible news. One of the most important items to keep track of is the budget. There are a variety of ways to approach the budget and we need to discuss a few of them.

First we have to answer the question, "Should you have a budget at all?" At first glance that may seem crazy but there may be some advantages in not having a budget. If, for example, the enemy spend less then you mentally budgeted for the wedding, you come out ahead.

Like the government or any large business, budgets are forecasted for the upcoming year and, without exception, all the money is spent. If the budget is not accurate, it is universally because more money is required, never that too much was allocated.

Therefore, before you sit down with the enemy to formulate a budget, try to determine which direction their preliminary plans are taking and make a decision about having a budget at all. Remember, you can always start out this way, sound like a big shot and tell the enemy not to worry about the money, and then later sit down and make a budget, when you realize things are getting out of control.

On the other hand, who are we kidding? You should have plenty of experience with your wife and daughter by now to know if this strategy has any chance of working. If you know it will not work, don't even start it; pick another option.

There are two main approaches to working out the budget. One is to come up with a bottom line figure, an amount above which the enemy cannot spend and let them determine how they want to allocate the money. This has some advantages, in that you can just sit back and not worry about the details. The disadvantage to this type of budget is that you can't worry about the details. Sometimes it's a good idea to worry about the details, so they don't get out of control. A series of decisions can be made that greatly exceeds the budget after you already become committed for the expense.

The other alternative is to develop a "line item" budget. List all of the major categories of expense and determine a budget for each of the items, still making sure that the total expense does not exceed a predetermined figure. In both cases, you had better determine what you can afford before you go through the exercise of budget making. You may not want to divulge your maximum figure to the enemy, but you better have one for yourself.

The line item budget gives you greater control over the individual expenses to ensure you do not exceed the overall maximum, but it does require greater supervision on your part. That means you will have to get involved more and increase your risk for confrontation, argument and ulcers.

What about budget shortfalls? Is it possible? Yes, you may be one of the fortunate few who find that your ideas were more grandiose than the enemy's and perhaps in one or two areas you were able to save a bit of money. What to do? You could be a sport and let them rearrange the budget taking the extra money and putting it into some other category. Or you could just keep the extra. You need to consider the pros and cons of your decision as it will affect your family and your future.

More likely than shortfalls will be budget overages. Smart budgeters will have considered the likelihood of this and padded the budget a bit to account for unexpected (or expected) overages. If not you have the unenviable task of finding more money to throw into the pot or refusing to allow the overages. The former may be hard, but the latter may be impossible.

Establishing the budget should be an early task. Many of the later decisions will impinge on the decision so that some discussion of the wedding details will have to precede the budget. For example, will the wedding reception be inside or outside, and if outside will there be a tent available in case of rain. Obviously, this decision will impact the budget figure. Nevertheless, as in all large scale operations, several issues may have to be discussed simultaneously. Just make sure one of the early decisions is the budget or everything will be much more expensive than you desire and can usually afford.

Once this onerous phase of the wedding is confronted and decisions completed then a great deal of your headache is over. Over, that is, if you make sure the budget is satisfactory and it is followed. Just remember the federal government. After all, your wife is the president, isn't she?

Let me share two important questions that deal with weddings such as yours. The first is: What are the "three s's" of the father of the bride? They are: Sit down, Shut up and Shell out. The second is: What are five words guaranteed to strike fear into the heart of the father of the bride? The answer is: "That's only the down payment!"

As the wedding date gets closer, you will find that these questions arise with increasing frequency. Right now they may sound cute. Just wait a few months.

CHECK LIST
The Budget

☐ Make a budget
☐ Make it early
☐ Make it realistic
☐ Double it
☐ Follow it
☐ Don't switch line items
☐ Don't increase the bottom line
☐ Keep any extra money
☐ Don't let your wife intimidate you

Setting The Date

Sounds easy, right? Besides, how can the date influence expenses of the wedding? ("Expenses are what I should be interested in and only expenses.") Wrong!

Setting the date for the wedding can be one of the most difficult and financially important decisions that must be made. I suppose the first consideration should be when the bride and groom want to (or have to) get married. Of course, their wishes are important, but may take second place to such things as availability of the church/synagogue, reception hall, band, or even the clergyperson.

First, consider the season. June is very popular. I wonder why? Perhaps because of the usually nice weather or the profusion of flowers that are in bloom, or because wedding planners like to ski in the winter. Nevertheless, if it must be June then you should plan very far ahead. The fringe benefit to planning for the distant future is the possibility that the couple may change their minds and elope or even call the whole thing off. Think of the money you will save.

In fact, every season has its proponents and opponents for the best time to have a wedding. In each season, you better worry about such things as inclement weather, especially if you are planning an outdoor wedding. Tents are not cheap to rent. Ice and snow can play havoc with entire wedding arrangements. And don't forget special weather problems in your area, such as hurricanes, earthquakes, or tornados. Since there are special problems regardless of the season involved, make sure you understand what they are and plan for them. In fact, as a general rule of thumb, plan for the worst; it probably will happen.

What about the day of the week? While there may be some religious restrictions, such as getting married on the Sabbath, almost any day of the week can be used for the ceremony. Want a small wedding? Plan it for a Monday night during football season. Want a smaller one? Plan it for Superbowl Sunday, or better yet, during any weekday at noon to conflict with the soap operas on television.

Financial impact? You bet. Somehow, weddings on Saturday evening seem to require bigger food and drink budgets. Sunday afternoons lend themselves more to a champagne and wedding cake affair. Time of day as well as day of the week all can play a role in your impending financial catastrophe.

Your job is to get the day and time you can afford, without appearing to want it for financial reasons. Maybe you can invoke some long-standing family tradition that you would like to carry on to the next generation. Perhaps you can find some obscure biblical reference to dictate a financially appropriate day and time. Just remember, the bible has been fairly well read and interpreted for a few thousand years. I couldn't find such a reference, but you should try it yourself. You can't do yourself any harm if you are seen studying the bible.

Once you are happy with the season, day and time of the wedding, remember that you will always run into conflicts. First, there is every likelihood that there will be another function which most of the guests you intended to invite also would want to attend. In fact, you might just want to attend the other function yourself. That could be good news or bad news. The bad news is you may have to miss the other function; the good news is that everyone you invite will go to the other function and you can have a small wedding. I wouldn't worry too much about either especially if the other function was planned first. You probably will have to choose a different date.

Even if there is no other conflicting function, there will be a certain number of people you have invited who will have personal conflicts and be unable to attend. In fact, you only may have about half the people you invite say "yes." Of course, with your luck, everyone you invite will want to come. After all they wouldn't want to miss the party of the year, so you're better off trying to influence exactly how many invitations are mailed.

Finally, of course, is the most important conflict. The one that is the most crucial and difficult to avoid: your weekly golf game! I don't know when you play, but I can assure you that it will be on the same day everyone else wants the wedding. This requires some difficult decision-making on your part. This is your favorite, only, or oldest daughter. You really do love her and want only the best for her. But your golf game—oh well, that will be your problem.

There is one thing you can count on. Once the date is set and other plans are made around that date, there will be precious little opportunity to change the decision. It may be the only one that won't change.

CHECK LIST
Setting the Date

❑ Consider the season
❑ Consider the weather
❑ Remember June is busy
❑ Consider the day of the week
❑ Consider the time of day
❑ Remember conflicts with other functions
❑ Remember conflicts with key participants
❑ Remember conflicts with your golf date
❑ Don't let your wife intimidate you

The Wedding Director

As the wedding day approaches, you can expect things to get a bit hectic. There will be a trillion things to do, any one of which, if forgotten, will absolutely destroy the entire occasion. The mother of the bride will try to keep track of these details. She will have fistfuls of paper, at least one book with instructions, notes and lists of things to do. She will be frazzled.

I know that by now you are also in a fairly desperate state. You have been abused, intimidated and had your own ancestry called into question by your wife. I suspect, at first glance, you have somewhat ambivalent feelings seeing you wife in such a state. Believe me, you better do something to help her or you will never stop paying the price.

There is an alternative. One of the best support systems to ensure a smooth running wedding is the wedding director. Your family needs a person who can manage all the details and do so in a calm and efficient manner. The wedding director can take all the worrisome details off your hands and make sure everything works out. She will make sure all the participants are in the correct place, that the flower girl has flowers, that the rings are at hand, that the bride's dress is arranged appropriately and that you know when to start walking down the aisle. In fact, the wedding director can make the whole affair reasonably tolerable for you. So, if your wife doesn't bring up the subject, you bring it up. The wedding director is worth the investment.

Do not fall into the trap of allowing a friend or relative to assume this position, thereby saving the expense. Wedding directors are not that expensive and you need one with experience in these matters. A wedding director has to possess the skills of a Marine drill sergeant combined with the tact of a marriage counselor.

When choosing a wedding director, use the same techniques as for the band or caterer. Ask for and check references. Perhaps you have attended a wedding where the director was involved and you know about her skills first hand. So much the better.

Then, after you have taken pains to choose the best director you can find, by all means, listen to and take her advice. After she has been involved with several weddings, she will learn all sorts of tricks to make sure things go smoothly. Remember the advisors we talked about before? They will surely advise differently than the director. You will be faced with two opposite opinions, one from an advisor and one from the director. The decision is easy: take the advice of the wedding director each and every time. You will not be sorry.

And don't make the mistake of using the wedding director only on the day of the wedding. These experts can give good advice all along the way. Remember, the advice will be given to the enemy and may, at times, be expensive. However, the wedding director should at least prevent dumb and inexperienced expenses. She will usually maintain some sort of reality based decision making. She also may know about a seamstress that can duplicate that dress at half the price and that the particular caterer you are considering consistently creates inedible food. The director may make your life and the whole affair significantly improved.

In other words, **SHE IS EASILY WORTH THE MONEY.** She is a good investment.

CHECK LIST
The Wedding Director

- ❏ Choose wedding director
  - Amateur (NO!)
  - Professional (YES!)
- ❏ Check credentials
- ❏ Check references
- ❏ Listen to her advice
- ❏ Take her advice
- ❏ Let her get involved early in the planning process
- ❏ Don't let your wife intimidate you

Location

Where are you going to have this wedding? Many factors come into play. First of all, what city should you choose? I suppose, if the bride and her family, the groom and his family and all the couple's friends live in the same city, the decision is easy. In today's society, this is not usually the case. Rather, all of these essential individuals live in different cities.

Traditionally (there's that word again) the wedding is held in the home city of the bride. I suppose it's fair, if the father of the bride is going to pay for the wedding and since that usually means the preponderance of the guests will be from the bride's side of the family.

Consider, if you will, the alternative. You, the father of the bride, adopt the position that you will be happy to pay for the wedding (thus limiting the groom's guests) but you think it most appropriate to have the wedding in the city of the groom's family. If you can pull that off you may have saved yourself considerable financial outlay by having a small wedding.

Well, it's just like the elopement trick. You can try it but it probably won't work. The wedding will be in your hometown, where you know just about everybody, do extensive business with all of them and cannot possibly insult them by excluding them from the party of the year.

Now that we answered that question, let's discuss where, in town, you are going to have the wedding. Again, not an easy decision. Actually there are two questions to answer here: where will you have the ceremony? and where will you have the reception?

Of course you can have both in the same place, but you need to consider all the possibilities. Most wedding ceremonies are held in a church or synagogue. Certainly such buildings lend themselves to the solemnity of the occasion. But considerations such as the availability of the specific church or synagogue you require, and the size of the sanctuary compared to the size of the guest list, are important. For these reasons, you may need to consider utilization of a church or synagogue different from your usual place of worship. For that matter, you may have the same problem with selection of the clergyperson. Certainly you would prefer your regular clergyperson, but he or she may be unavailable or may not be able to perform the ceremony in a borrowed building.

Of course, ceremonies can really be performed anywhere. A hotel ballroom or reception hall can serve the purpose. One of the most moving ceremonies I ever attended was held in a country club reception hall, suitably decorated to resemble an outside wedding, with lots of tiny twinkling lights representing stars.

Many prefer an actual outside ceremony in a beautiful setting, perhaps near a beach or garden. I have it on very good authority that, regardless of the location, there is every probability the prayers and declarations made by the bride and groom will be heard and blessed.

Please remember that if an outside wedding is chosen, there had better be a contingency for inclement weather. You better have either a suitable size (and expensive) tent available or an appropriate building nearby to use in an emergency.

Well, father of the bride, virtually any option will cost you, but this is a necessary expense and will not be the end of your fortune. Most churches or synagogues are reasonably priced. The use of a hotel may even be free—since you will be buying many items and services from the hotel, anyway. Reception halls can be expensive, so be wary if this is your choice. In addition to a basic rental fee, many additional items may be added, such as a fee for the use of the kitchen, parking and other amenities. These charges are unavoidable and unless you plan to use Yankee Stadium your expenses will be determined more by the other decisions about the wedding.

Some couples prefer the bizarre. We have all heard about weddings held in unusual places, depending on the whims and interests of the bride and groom. Ceremonies at the bottom of the ocean at one extreme, a hot air balloon at the other and everything else in between have been tried. If the bride and groom need to be innovative, encourage it. Weddings in strange places are usually small and inexpensive. How many wedding guests can fit into a telephone booth or a submarine?

There is one other option that should be mentioned because I believe it is becoming more popular. Some couples choose a location totally separate from anybody's home town. Consider packing up everyone who will go and have a wedding in Israel, at some holy place. Regardless of your beliefs, there are a multitude of religious shrines scattered around Israel that would provide a motivating background for the ceremony.

And let's not forget a secular setting, particularly if the ceremony will not be performed by a clergyperson. You know that a variety of individuals, including judges and ship captains, are allowed to perform the ceremony. This greatly expands the options for finding a suitable or unique setting.

Now we have to add another variable into the equation: the reception. Again, there are a wide variety of choices. Remember, almost every church or synagogue has a reception or activity hall and depending on the desired ambiance and size, it could serve very well for the reception. On the other hand, if the ceremony is somewhere other than a house of worship then other sites for the reception will be required. Still a very popular site is a hotel or reception hall, especially if that's the location of the ceremony. Obviously the expenses involved with a reception in a hotel probably will be greater than in a church or synagogue, but believe me, a creative enemy can find ways to decorate any site and fill it with enough food and drinks to bankrupt Rockefeller.

In most cases (besides the size and location requirements of the reception site), other factors will be considered by the enemy. Be ready for just about anything. How about, "I like the room, but the carpet is the wrong color?" Or, "I want to be able to see the ocean from the reception hall windows?" Or, "The room is nice but there aren't enough bathrooms?" Some of the considerations may sound crazy to you, but they may decide your financial future.

I offered to bring in Porta-Potties. Just imagine how my suggestion went over. My best advice is to keep a low profile on this decision, as there are some really big ones coming up and you can't afford to use all your ammunition on this one.

CHECK LIST
Location

- ❑ Choose the city where:
    - You live
    - The bride lives
    - The groom lives
    - The groom's family live
    - Somewhere in between
    - Some foreign country
- ❑ Choose the church or synagogue
- ❑ Choose the hotel or reception hall
- ❑ Choose an indoor or outdoor site
- ❑ Don't let your wife intimidate you

Guests

We are now about to talk "real business." Choosing the wedding date and location is important, but determining the number of guests to be invited can make or break you. It is not a complicated matter. Whatever you select for the style or lavishness of the reception, the more people attending, the more it costs.

Early on, you will be accosted with lists of potential guests. Your daughter will have a list of her friends, the groom will have a list, and they probably will have a third list of mutual friends. The father and mother of the groom also will have a list. Your wife will have a list, and there probably will be one or two people you would like to invite yourself.

Even if you all have lived in the same community all your lives and even if the bride and groom have known each other for years, it's amazing how the lists will differ and none will contain the same people. So don't expect to reduce each of the lists in half because they have common names.

Are you going to invite everybody on all the lists? If you do, the rest of this section is superfluous. Otherwise, you need some strategies to come up with reasonable compromises. It will not be easy, since each of the lists has already been scrutinized by the enemy to make them as "short as possible," only inviting "those who are absolutely necessary."

There is a bit of good news, if you are very lucky. It is very unlikely that everyone on the invitation list will be able to attend. There doesn't even have to be a major conflicting function the same time as the wedding. Some people will be out of town, on a cruise or sight-seeing abroad. In fact, a rule of thumb is that only about 60% of those invited will accept. Remember, that's the usual case. There will be some tense days after the invitations go out and before you can be sure who will attend.

You may want to consider limiting everyone's list to an arbitrary number. In order to do this appropriately you had better have a good idea of your overall budget and what the major items involved will cost. The reception hall probably will cost the same despite the number invited unless you go from one extreme to the other. But the caterer will have a good deal to say about the various costs for different numbers of guests.

Be careful. Do you really want to tell your new in-laws that they can't invite all those "necessary" people? Hopefully these new family members will be around for a long time and you want to maintain the best possible relationship with them. Start off on the right foot.

The bride and groom will feel quite protective of invitations for their friends. They may ask you who the wedding is really for, anyway. They probably won't understand that the party is for family and friends of you and your wife and that the wedding is only the excuse to return all those social obligations that you have incurred in the past, when you were invited out and never reciprocated with an invitation of your own.

Naturally, the mother of the bride will not have anything to do with your lame excuses about limiting her own guest list. You might as well not even try it with her.

The bottom line is that it may be better to try to save money elsewhere in the wedding process and just bite the bullet and invite the correct number of people. The correct number is everyone on every list. The risk of permanent enmity is so great that your future will really look bleak if you try anything else.

Perhaps a few words about children are in order. You may want to consider limiting or eliminating the presence of small children at the wedding. Some people like to bring infants along with them to both the ceremony and reception. Small children have a propensity to cry, usually at just the wrong times. Toddlers like to toddle and youngsters often like to participate in the service by mimicking the priest, minister or rabbi, usually in a very loud voice. Telling any youngster to be quiet is futile. The enemy probably will handle this decision for you, but consider whether you want any input into the argument.

There are a few other pitfalls. Don't even think that you can try inviting some people to the ceremony without inviting them to the reception. That's the best way I know to produce lifelong enemies. You can do it the other way, and invite a lot of guests to the reception, after you have a "small, family ceremony." That doesn't achieve much in the way of cost savings, although there may be some personal reasons why that may be appropriate.

You could try to limit the length of the reception by noting both a starting time and a finishing time on the invitation, but most people ignore such statements and the major expense of the reception occurs in the beginning, not at the end.

Finally, you can forego the reception altogether. Try it. If you figure out how to do that, please let me know. Remember, there is a time to smile and accept your fate. I suppose there is also a time to "draw a line in the sand" and go no further, but I'm not sure the risk is worth it.

CHECK LIST
Guests

- ☐ Make a list
- ☐ Make several lists, one for each event
- ☐ Limit the lists
- ☐ Keep the number on each list low
- ☐ Try for a "family only" wedding
- ☐ Schedule the wedding on Super Bowl Sunday
- ☐ Don't invite children
- ☐ Don't invite people you hate
- ☐ Learn to hate a lot of people
- ☐ Remember, everyone invited won't come
- ☐ Don't let your wife intimidate you

Invitations

This brings us to invitations. No, a telephone call invitation will not suffice. A newspaper advertisement will certainly not be appropriate. Even a nice, personal, handwritten note will not be satisfactory. You will have to have printed or engraved invitations prepared and mailed far enough in advance to allow the guests to make appropriate arrangements.

By the way, we do need to mention what your wedding invitation will do to those lucky individuals who will attend. The lucky husband will have the opportunity to have his wife go out and get a new outfit for the occasion. Naturally, a dress, shoes and other accessories will be essential. After all, this will be quite a social occasion and she cannot be expected to appear in anything but the finest. I'm sure the husbands invited will be happy to do this and thank you for the opportunity. They also may have to cancel their golf games or give up that important program on television. Worse yet, they have to get dressed up themselves, put on that shirt with the stiff collar and probably a tie as well.

Back to the invitations: they have to be printed. They may have a design of some type or at least set the theme for the wedding. Yes, weddings can have themes. I went to one recently that featured Cajun cuisine and had a Mardi Gras look. Of course, the invitations will have to be contained in an envelope within the mailing envelope. I don't know why, but they do. The envelope probably will have to have a lining. Again, I don't know why. Cards will be inserted so that the invited guests can respond to the invitation. They also will need a return envelope with a stamp already attached.

There also may have to be other inserts, perhaps with directions and maps to the ceremony or reception. Somewhere in the whole thing is a piece of tissue paper, probably there so you don't get tears on the invitations when you are mailing them.

If by any strange chance it becomes your job to mail the invitations, and you have to buy stamps, you better be careful to choose appropriate postage stamps, something with love on them.

What about addressing the invitations? Well you can pay a bit extra and have your return address printed on the envelope. Or you can write out both addresses by hand, but it's not that simple. The enemy may want the invitations to look really "classy" and insist that the addresses be written in calligraphy. That translates into very ornate, hand drawn works of art that usually are quite expensive unless you know someone who does calligraphy for a hobby and is a very good friend.

By the way, if you have done all this, you better determine how much postage is required since the whole package may be very heavy. No, even if it can qualify for bulk mailing, the enemy won't let you do it.

CHECK LIST
Invitations

❑ Avoid expensive invitations—do you save your invitations?
❑ Buy more than you think you need
❑ Practice your calligraphy
❑ Pick out "love" stamps
❑ Send invitations out early enough. If too late—guests may have other commitments and may not be able to attend (hint)
❑ Frame one, it may be all you have left
❑ Don't let your wife intimidate you

Rehearsal Dinner

Here is a bit of good news. (I think it's important to tell you the good news as well as the bad news.) Although you will find much more bad news than good news, you should read this.

There will be a rehearsal for this wedding. You know that everyone, including you, must learn how and when to walk, sit and participate in the ceremony. You have an especially important part in this production. You will not only have the honor of walking the bride down the aisle, but you will actually get the chance to "give her away." Please understand that you are not really giving her away in the permanent sense. You will never get rid of her. I'm sure you don't really want to, anyway: she is your daughter. But the symbolic gesture you will make at the ceremony has to be done correctly.

Now, after the rehearsal, there will usually be a dinner. Originally, they tell me, this dinner was for the members of the wedding party. It was usually a small affair, with a meal, some toasts to the bride and groom and home early so that everyone could have a good night's sleep to be ready for the next day's festivities.

Somewhere along the line the emphasis changed to include not only the wedding party but all the out-of-town guests. In some cases that could be almost the entire guest list for the wedding itself. Again, depending on the wishes of the enemy, the affair can become quite lavish, and include drinks, dinner and dancing.

But, the good news is that the rehearsal dinner is the responsibility of the groom, or at least his side of the family. Both families had better have some discussion about the details of the arrangements, but this does not come out of your traditional pocket, or at least your checkbook.

If you are going to be responsible for the wedding day festivities, I guess it is appropriate for the groom's side to take care of the rehearsal dinner. Of course, If you have arrived at some other arrangement with the groom's family for the wedding and reception, then you better be consistent with the financial arrangements for the rehearsal dinner as well. Under certain circumstances both functions may almost equal each other, but before you get too smug about the whole thing, this is the exception, rather than the rule and the wedding will be the greater financial burden, by far.

CHECK LIST
Rehearsal Dinner

❑ Remember, the groom pays
❑ Remember, the groom's family plans
❑ Choose guests for the rehearsal dinner
       Wedding party only
       All "out of town" guests
       Everybody–and call it the wedding
❑ Don't forget the rehearsal itself
❑ At the rehearsal, do whatever you are told
❑ Don't volunteer suggestions
❑ Don't let your wife intimidate you

The Ceremony

The ceremony is often the most neglected portion of the entire wedding operation. To put it into perspective, which is more important, the decision about serving spicy chicken wings or the decision about the prayers to be read? Oh, don't get me wrong, countless hours may be spent in discussing the ceremony, but that time is usually spent arguing about the color of the bridesmaids' dresses.

There are certainly major fiscal implications of the ceremony, as we shall discuss, but there are also many decisions that have to be made that have little financial effect. It is a very good strategy to get the enemy so engrossed in the non-financial decisions that they forget the financial ones. Good luck!

If the wedding is going to be in a church or synagogue an entirely different ceremony will take place than if the wedding is going to be performed by a judge or ship captain. Even though the decision has been made to have a religious ceremony many other decisions will have to be made. Will you have a standard, official ceremony where all the rituals are prescribed? Or, will you modify the standard ritual to make it more personal or even write your own ceremony? Clergypersons vary on the latitude they are willing to give the wedding couple to modify the ceremony, but many beautiful services have been individually written. Admittedly, some unusual services have also been performed.

Just the subject of music can consume hours of discussion and decision making. A church organ is nice, but how about other instruments: violins, guitars, trumpets, or the whole orchestra? How about a vocalist, and what will he or she sing? Processional and recessional choices abound.

Of course the church or synagogue will have to be decorated with flowers and other ornaments. Certainly the standard house of worship decor will be insufficient for your wedding.

The Gown

And now we come to the expensive part—clothing. What will the bride wear? The only thing already decided is that her dress will be white. You know about the tradition of why white is chosen for the bride. Please remember this is the late twentieth century. If that were an absolute rule there probably would be only one or two white dresses sold in a year.

The bridal gown probably will be the single most expensive purchase of the entire wedding plan. You probably will spend more for food, but as a single item purchase, you won't beat the bride's outfit. Again, choices have to be made. Perhaps you think your daughter can go into a ready made bridal store and pick out the first gown she sees and buy it? Wrong! There will be many dresses to choose from and she will want to try them all. Some have lace, some tulle (whatever that is) some even have pearls sewn on them and some of them are real pearls. Choosing a dress will be a complicated affair.

In fact, there may be many dresses not to choose from, since one can be designed specifically for your bride. Bridal dress designers are available in most high quality stores. I hate to mention names like Neiman-Marcus or Bloomingdales' or Saks Fifth Avenue but I know that these stores will be happy to arrange a custom made dress for your daughter. By the way, it does help if your daughter or someone in your immediate family works in that store and can get an employee discount. But even with the discount, watch out!

Here's a good idea: pick out the dress she likes the best, get photographs of it and have it copied by a talented seamstress. Now, I did say talented because a poorly made dress will make everyone unhappy. Nevertheless, a well made copy could really save you money. The dress is only worn for a few hours and will then probably be stored away forever. Do you really remember your wife's wedding dress?

As a matter of fact, speaking of your wife's wedding dress, do you remember how you paid all that money to have the dress heirloomed and stored away? Do you remember where it is in the attic or top of the closet? Have you considered trying to suggest that it would be a nice touch if your daughter wore the same dress your wife did? I tried it, but it didn't work for me.

I am sure, with our luck, that if they did decide to try it after all these years they would have opened the sealed box and found nothing but a small pile of dust where the dress had been. Besides, styles have changed and the "something borrowed" was never meant to mean the wedding gown.

So get ready for an expensive dress, even if copied. And, of course, there is the matter of the headpiece, veil, shoes, underclothing and, naturally, the garter, probably the cheapest article of all.

If you are really a "bum" try to suggest renting a wedding dress, just as you would rent a tuxedo for yourself. Why go to all that expense when you could save the money for something important? In fact, you can not only rent wedding dresses but appropriate dresses for the entire wedding party. Somehow, I don't think you'll be able to pull it off.

The Wedding Party

That brings us to the rest of the wedding party. The bride and groom will want a certain number of their friends and family to participate in the wedding ceremony and help them with the whole affair. I have been to weddings that include only a maid of honor and a best man in the party. But I have also been to weddings where up to a dozen bridesmaids and a matching set of groomsmen all participate. Thankfully, this will not be your decision, although there may be some financial impact on you, in addition to just increasing the number of guests. We will talk about that later when we discuss gifts that have to be given. That's right, given. It's not just gifts received anymore. Anyway, the number of bridesmaids and groomsmen will have to be determined. The number will have to be equal and include all the many "closest" friends the bridal couple has as well as brothers or sisters, if they exist. This can be a vexing decision. Obviously, there cannot be twenty or thirty individuals standing near the bridal couple. Such a number would detract from the bride. How can insulting several close friends or family be avoided? It may not be easy.

Once the number is determined, the next big decision is what the bridesmaids will wear. This has major implications for the entire wedding, since they will have to match the colors chosen for the wedding. Colors? That's right, colors. I'm sure you know that every wedding you've ever been to is color coordinated. Perhaps the bride's favorite color will be the main theme carried through the clothing, flowers and decorations. Your daughter has always known what color she wants for her wedding. She may have not realized it before, but I believe it is genetically determined, this time, by your wife's genes.

A color will be chosen and the female members of the wedding party will be clothed in that color. Then a particular, standardized dress will be chosen for all the women to wear. Your wife and daughter probably will choose a dress that compliments no one and that will never be worn at any place other than your wedding. This is so that the bridesmaids can purchase such a dress and never use it again. By the way, these dresses are not cheap. Do the ladies in the wedding party a favor and try to influence the enemy to choose a dress that can be used elsewhere. It probably won't work, but at least your conscience will be clear.

Accessories such as shoes, jewelry and even such issues as hairdos will be determined and forced on these bridesmaids, without their input in the decision. But don't feel too badly for them, as they will have their own weddings and be able to do the same for their bridal party, which probably will include your daughter. Just hope that they get married after your wedding, so that you won't have to pay for your daughter's outfit: your son-in-law can take care of that problem.

The groom will choose his outfit and the outfits of his groomsmen. As I reread that sentence I see how silly it sounds. He won't choose anything. The enemy will tell him what to wear and what his party will wear. It probably will be some type of formal attire that can be rented. Even though the rental fee will be exorbitant, it will still be infinitely cheaper then the ladies' dresses. Do not think that just because you already own a tuxedo it will be suitable for the wedding. You, the father of the bride, will have to be coordinated with the rest of the wedding party and your old, out of style and off color suit will not match.

In addition to the maid of honor (matron, if married), best man, bridesmaids and groomsmen, there will be several other members of the wedding party that will have to be chosen and clothed. Do not forget the mother of the bride. Your wife probably will want a new outfit for the festivities. I'll guarantee she has no dress anywhere near the color that has been chosen for the wedding. The grandparents of the bride also will have to be considered as well as the flower girls, ring bearers and anyone else included in the wedding party.

Then, of course, there are the guests. A decision will have to be made that could affect or strain your relationship with your friends for life. Perhaps the enemy will want to add two words to the invitation that could convert your friends to life long enemies. "BLACK TIE" could do it. If it going to be a fancy affair, especially in the evening, it may please your wife and daughter to make this choice. Remember, black tie means that the men will have to wear tuxedos, which they may or may not have, but it also means the women can go out and buy a new formal outfit and blame you for making them do it. Do you see your problem?

Ceremony Problems

We have not yet discussed the complicated parts of this wedding. I doubt all of these problems will occur, simply because we have discussed them. Rather some new ones will appear, just to confuse and confound you. Nevertheless, a myriad of problems can, and will, occur when dealing with the ceremony. Here are only a few.

The church or synagogue may be too small. They may have had a fire in it, just last week. The clergyperson may become ill. Someone in the wedding party will be unable to attend, thereby unbalancing the number of men and women. The flower girl will get a cold. A blizzard will close the roads. It will rain on your outdoor wedding. If you have a tent, for just such an emergency, it will leak and will not be large enough. Someone will forget the wedding book so that no one can sign in. The candles will ignite the ferns. The amplification system will break and no one will hear or understand the ceremony.

It goes on and on. If everything works correctly, it will not be because of great planning, but will only be another sign of divine intervention. Weddings are joyous occasions.

CHECK LIST
Ceremony, Gown, Wedding Party, Ceremony Problems

☐ Don't forget to show up
☐ Keep it short
☐ Smile a lot
☐ Look proud
☐ Feel proud
☐ Remember you're not losing a daughter
☐ Remember you're gaining a son
☐ Choose style of ceremony
☐ Choose music
☐ Choose ritual
    Standard
    Modified
    Bizarre
☐ Buy a nice wedding dress
☐ Try to get a dress copied
☐ Avoid use of the word "designer"
☐ Try to get the bride to wear a "rental"
☐ Try to find out what "tulle" is
☐ Choose bridal party clothing that can be worn for other uses
☐ Consider your guests when you specify "black tie"
☐ Choose flowers and decorations
☐ Try to get them used at the reception as well
☐ Call weather service frequently, if the wedding is outdoors
☐ Prepare contingency plans (i.e., tent)
☐ Don't let your wife intimidate you

The Reception

Everything before this has been peanuts. Now comes the real action, the reception. Sure, you can do it cheaply. As a matter of fact, a reception that includes only champagne for toasting and a cake for good luck can be a marvelous affair. Not only that, if that's all you can afford, then that's all you should do.

But, let's be honest. John Paul Getty will not be able to have such a reception. Will you? Now that we have that out of the way let's talk seriously.

Where will you have the reception? We have discussed some of this already, but we need to consider some more details. There are a variety of choices including the reception hall of the church or synagogue. Many of them are quite nicely arranged and decorated, They usually have associated kitchen facilities for food preparation, stages for music and so on. One of the major advantages of such an arrangement is the convenience of not having to travel to the reception from the ceremony. If the facilities are adequate, this option has much to recommend it. By the way, whatever the church or synagogue charges for the use of the room, it will be far less than a commercial reception hall will charge.

A hotel or reception hall is another alternative. Try to find one that will meet you needs and still not be located in another city or county so that travel can be minimized. Discuss the financial arrangements with the management carefully and be sure you understand all the intricacies of the contract. There will usually be a set fee for use of the room. If it is a hotel, they may waive the fee since you are purchasing other services, such as food, from them. In fact, insist they waive the fee. A reception hall may add other charges to the usual fee, such as a cleanup fee and a kitchen use fee based on the number of guests attending. Bar set up fees, in addition to drinks, may be charged. You also may be charged for use of tables, chairs, linen such as tablecloths and napkins and anything else the management can think of to take your money. Study the contract carefully. Be sure you know, in advance, what you will have to pay.

Another possibility for the site for the reception could be a beautiful outdoor setting among gardens or in a park. This can be gorgeous but also present logistical difficulties including food preparation, food service, weather conditions such as wind or rain and the

unwanted presence of creepy crawly bugs and other animals. You should have an alternate plan should difficulties arise.

Finally, if the reception will be separate from the ceremony, plan ahead about the transportation from one to the other. The bride and groom can ride in a limousine, although a variation such as a horse drawn carriage is a nice touch. The rest of the bridal party has to be moved and should go as a group instead of using their own individual transportation. Perhaps a limo, or bus, or some original form of transportation would be in order. Try to make it smooth and efficient. There will be a significant delay after the ceremony anyway, because photographs of the bridal party are usually taken. Since most of the guests will want to start eating and drinking at the reception, transportation problems can only result in further delays.

It is also a good idea to check out parking facilities at the reception before committing to a signed contract. Nothing is more frustrating than to have so little off street parking that it becomes difficult for the guests to get into the building. Valet parking is a good alternative when off street parking is limited, but is more expense.

Let's talk about food and drinks. (This is where it gets exciting.) You will need to supply both, in profuse quantities. When the guests arrive at the reception, usually well before the bridal party, you will have to keep them busy, and the best way to do this is with something to drink and a bite to eat. Decisions you make here will set the tone for the rest of the reception.

Clearly the most lavish is to provide every type of drink imaginable including wine, beer, champagne and distilled spirits. No one will really expect the fancy mixed drinks such as a frozen frufru but margaritas, manhattans and martinis would be nice. Since you have now gone into the bar business you better remember what all tavern owners know so well: be very careful about accounting for all liquor consumed. You may have to purchase your own liquor since some reception halls or caterers do not do this. If so, arrange to get more than you need with the clear understanding that you can return unopened bottles. Then make sure that the bartenders don't open a new bottle until the old one is used. It will be impossible, but try to keep track of it.

It is not essential that all possible types of alcoholic beverages are served, or that the most expensive brands used. This is a decision that you will have to make. Remember that certain religions actually forbid the use of alcoholic beverages at any time, and I have never seen any members of such religious groups look seriously deprived because of their abstinence. While you do not have to eliminate serving such drinks to the guests at the reception, you may want to consider a conversion so that you can claim you are only serving a fruit punch because of your own religious convictions. You look bad if you reconvert back to your original religious preferences immediately after the wedding.

Whatever your choice of beverage served, do make sure you have enough on hand to satisfy all the guests. Try to estimate the quantities you will need based on the time during which the drinks will be served. The caterer will be happy to help you in this regard. Also remember that if some of your guests do not want to drink alcoholic beverages, it is essential that you have some alternatives available. Soft drinks are popular. The diet variety is increasingly demanded and is an inexpensive alternative.

That brings us to food. Most guests will want to eat a bite while they are drinking and awaiting the arrival of the bridal party. Appetizers can be served and do make a nice touch, and if you will be having a separate dinner after a cocktail period then they are almost a must. If you intend to blend the cocktail period with the serving of a buffet type of food service then it is not so important. So the basic decision is, will you have a separate meal?

But this basic decision creates lots more decisions. Will the meal be a sit down type dinner with the food served by waiters and waitresses? This is a very nice affair, but will be expensive since so many employees will be required. The meal can include soup, salad, an entree and dessert. You can get as fancy as you want and include several more courses including a sorbet to clear you palate between courses. Two, or more, types of wine are nice, the choice depending on the choice of the different courses. In fact, a few desserts wouldn't be a bad idea in case your guests have different tastes. I have even been to weddings that served sumptuous meals but also included a bagel to "nosh" on the trip home.

If you choose the sit down dinner, then you have to decide where everyone will sit. Of course, you can leave the decision to the guests themselves, but this usually results in a mad dash, as soon as the doors are opened, for everyone to get a seat, and even to guests forming "table pools" so they can sit together. The alternative is to designate the tables with numbers and provide each guest with a corresponding numbered card so that they sit in designated seats.

You will have to plan carefully who will sit where. A large number of variables will have to be considered, since you can only put a certain number of guests at any given table. You will have to worry about such factors as who is currently angry with whom, are the strangers at the same table compatible, will you insult Aunt Sadie by putting her too far away from the brides table, or Uncle Joe too close to the music? Many hours of fun and games can be consumed by these types of discussions and decisions. When you are done with this jig saw puzzle, you will have invariably left someone out or insulted someone else.

You may reduce the cost of the catering by having a buffet instead of a sit down dinner. But there are some caterers who will point out that you may not save much because what you do save on servers will be spent on the food itself, since guests will no doubt serve themselves larger portions then would be served to them. If you do choose buffet type service be sure that there are enough serving lines so that your guests do not spend half the night waiting to get their food. Nothing is more frustrating to a natural born eater then to wait eternally to "go through the line."

Another problem encountered in some buffet type food service is the unavailability of sufficient tables and chairs for everyone. In a sit down dinner, by definition, there has to be a place for each guest. With a buffet type of meal, this is not always done and some guests may be forced to eat with the plate in their laps or some other inconvenient place, perhaps balancing the plate on a shelf or railing.

By this time I'm sure you are rethinking the whole decision about even having a reception, but all is not lost. You do have a vendor (see "The Enemy") who will be happy to help you with all the details. Of course, you had better be sure of the vendor you have chosen. It is essential that you choose the caterer carefully. The guests probably will not recall the details of the clergyperson's sermon, or the color of the bridal gown, but they will certainly remember, in great detail, the quality of the food served.

Insist on, and check, several references before you hire the caterer. Once the menu has been selected, arrange to taste samples of the food. Be sure the caterer understands the necessity of not running out of food during the reception. Sometimes you may be able to sneak a visit to some other function the caterer has prepared and see just how it looks. The appearance of the food is important and so is the taste. It goes without saying that hot foods should be hot and cold foods cold. Be sure the caterer knows how to do that. Make sure the caterer is familiar with the reception hall and its facilities. Hopefully he or she has catered functions there before.

One of the decisions relating to the choice of the reception location is the issue of the caterer. If you choose a hotel, you get the food from the hotel. Make sure it is of the quality you desire. Here it is easier to taste and determine the quality of the food beforehand.

Regardless, choose the menu with care. I'm sure you want food items that are distinctive and unusual. Just make sure the caterer has had experience preparing these foods before and it may be better to go with what the caterer knows best. In any case, if the menu includes ethnic foods make sure you taste them first. And, if the wedding reception has special requirements related to the religious beliefs of the family, such as Kosher food, you better make sure the caterer can provide the necessary cuisine.

You may want to consider the choice of foods designed to be healthy as well as tasty. That seems to be all the rage and remember, chicken or fish is cheaper than prime rib. Make sure your guests know that you are really thinking about their health and not your pocketbook. Ho! Ho! Ho!

At some point before the wedding, the caterer will want a count of the number of guests who will be at the reception so that the appropriate amount of food can be purchased and prepared. Since the caterer has been there before (make sure of this—you don't want this to be his or her first job) there will be some extra food prepared, but not that much. If you overestimate the number of guests, there will be plenty of food, but you will be expected to pay for the number you guaranteed will be present. If you underestimate the number of guests you may have to issue that age old warning to the appropriate people: FHB (family hold back). Don't put yourself in that position. You won't like it.

The Cake

Central to the entire reception is the cake. I should say cakes because current tradition calls for a bride's and a groom's cake. The bride's cake will usually be a multi-tiered affair, the size determined in part by the number of guests that will partake of it. The uppermost layer is usually removed, frozen and eaten by the bride and groom on their first anniversary, for good luck. The remainder is cut and distributed to the guests for a dessert.

There will be a cake. Countless hours will be spent discussing the type of cake, the frosting and the decorations. Traditionally the top of the cake includes a small bride and groom decoration, but instead fresh or frosted flowers may be placed on top and, for that matter, all over the cake. I have even seen little lights twinkling on the cake as well as edible chocolate leaves and other designs. Wedding cakes can be purchased from bakeries, designed by cake designers who do nothing else or made by a member of the family or close friend, who can give it that personal touch.

It is important to make sure the cake, both inside and out is to your liking. Tasting the type of cake you will use beforehand is essential to be sure you are satisfied with the taste. Almost any type of cake can be used but try to prevent the enemy from choosing a cake that is clearly so unusual as to be bizarre.

Traditionally the groom's cake leaves a bit more latitude as to type and design of cake. It is an opportunity for the groom to express his individuality. Often chocolate, it can be in any imaginable shape or with any imaginable decoration. I have seen cakes fashioned with a school seal, especially if the groom is particularly proud of his university. Animal shapes seem to be quite popular, especially if the groom is an animal. (Ask the bride for advice here.) The bottom line is just about anything short of obscene goes for the groom's cake and even a little obscenity probably will pass.

Just make sure you like the cake's taste and design, but don't dispute the need for the cake itself.

Music

How could there be a wedding without music? I can't recall a wedding ceremony that did not include music at some point. The bridal procession, the bride and groom leaving together, a soloist or instrumental composition somewhere in the service or the chanting of prayers all help make the ceremony memorable. What about music at the reception? If you can afford it, it will add to the festivities.

Perhaps a harpist, perhaps a tinkling piano, but most guests would like to dance, particularly at an evening affair. Picking a band is like picking a caterer. You have to listen to the music and make sure it is to your liking. There are all types of musical ensembles playing all types of music. You have to have a plan to get through the maze.

First, decide what type of music you want. Jazz, rock, big band sound or whatever, make sure you take into account the predictable likes and dislikes of your guests, then make sure the band is conversant with that type of music. Listen to them. The size of the musical group will, in part, determine the cost. Obviously, the sound of the music will vary if the numbers vary, with larger groups sounding fuller and, some say, better.

Most groups can add members to their ranks if you want a larger sound, but it may be difficult to reduce their normal size and still get music. Take into consideration the size and type of reception hall in which the group will play. There is no doubt that with modern amplification systems any group can "fill" the room with music, but you do want to leave room for the guests and if the music is objectionable to them, they may find a way to leave the festivities early, thereby defeating your purpose.

Besides size, the cost of the musical groups varies with their own sense of value. A little known group of five will not cost you as much as The Beatles, if they were still around and if you could get them. Some groups will have agents that will negotiate for them and most every group feels they are unique and qualified to receive the highest fee.

But there is something about live music that will "make" the affair and anything less will be everything less. In addition, the leader can provide additional emcee type services during the reception. He or she can introduce the bride and groom, announce the cutting of the cake, throwing of the bouquet and the bride and groom's first dance; make sure your band leader is comfortable providing this service. If there is special music you desire, make sure the band will be able to play it.

Finally, if there is ethnic music or traditions involved with the reception, make sure the leader is thoroughly familiar with the music and when it is to be played. Entertainers can be "hams," and may find it hard to admit they don't know. Make sure!

Reception Rituals

Let's talk a little about the reception rituals. They won't cost you much but they have to be done. I'm not sure why but tradition dictates. (There's that tradition again.)

The bride and groom will have the first dance. They will dance to their favorite tune and will then ask the other members of the wedding party to dance, in order of seniority. You are pretty senior, so get ready. Make sure you can dance to the music. You better practice.

Toasts need to be made. The groom may make one, or perhaps the best man, but you better be ready yourself. The enemy will expect something sentimental and dealing with the happy couple, long life and all that sort of stuff. Practice your toast.

The cake will have to be cut, and the bride will have to feed a piece to the groom and vice versa. I don't know why, but it has to be done. They also will drink a glass of champagne together, and there will have to be special goblets for this.

The bride must throw the bouquet so that one of the unmarried women can catch it; it's the way that the next bride is determined. Do you think this has ever worked out? I doubt it. If you paid a fortune for the bridal bouquet and you intend to preserve it (yes, that can be done just as the dress can be preserved) then you better make sure the bride throws a different bouquet over her shoulder. After all, it may be trampled beneath the feet of hoards of attacking women who want to catch it or beneath the feet of the same women trying to run away from it. Your florist can make you a "throw down" bouquet which may be where that term came from anyway.

Then the garter has to follow. The groom will take the garter from you know where, and throw it over his shoulder to the waiting bachelors. Again, the lucky fellow who catches it is supposed to get married next. Pretty lucky, huh?

Depending on the circumstances there also may be other traditional ritualistic practices during the reception. Jewish weddings have special circle dancing, called the Hora. In addition, the bride and groom may be placed in chairs hoisted into the air and carried about by guests in time to the music. This stems from an ancient Hascedic tradition, but seems to be included in all Jewish wedding receptions regardless of the degree of orthodoxy.

Finally, after all the planning and paying, remember that this is a joyous occasion, and you might as well enjoy it yourself. Forget the cost, you have worried enough about the deposits before the wedding and you will worry plenty about the rest of the bills after the wedding. At least you can enjoy the wedding festivities themselves.

CHECK LIST
The Reception, Cake, Music, Rituals

❑ Prepare for all contingencies
❑ Choose location of reception
❑ Consider church or synagogue reception hall
❑ Choose hotel
❑ Get hotel to waive fee for room rental
❑ Check fee for use of kitchen
❑ Check fee for clean up
❑ Check fee for parking
❑ Check fee for bar set up
❑ Check fee for table set up
❑ Check fee for anything else they can think up
❑ Consider reception hall
❑ Consider outside site
❑ Check transportation and parking facilities
❑ Choose caterer and food
❑ Consider buffet dinner
❑ Ensure sufficient table and chairs
❑ Ensure sufficient lines to get food to minimize wait
❑ Consider sit down dinner
❑ Remember, sit down dinners are expensive
❑ Determine seating arrangement. Prepare to insult everyone
❑ Consider no dinner. Serve cake and champagne only
❑ Determine if reception site has a kitchen
❑ Determine the need for special foods or diets for any guests
❑ Make sure there is enough food
❑ Determine an accurate "count" for the caterer
❑ Choose drinks
❑ Consider a full bar with a complete array of liquor
❑ Make sure you can return unopened bottles
❑ Consider wine and beer only

- ❏ Make sure there is enough of whatever you decide to serve
- ❏ Choose cakes
    Standard type wedding cake
    Cakes unusual in either recipe, decorations or shapes
- ❏ Choose music
- ❏ Consider size of band and types of instruments
- ❏ Consider style of music to be played
- ❏ Consider disco
- ❏ Determine if there is a stage and other equipment for musicians
- ❏ Prepare usual wedding reception rituals
- ❏ Practice dancing
- ❏ Practice toasts
- ❏ Act like a gracious host
- ❏ Don't let your wife intimidate you

Flowers and Decorations

Flowers and brides are almost synonymous. They just go together. It doesn't matter where the wedding ceremony takes place, even if it's in a flower garden or greenhouse, extra flowers will be required.

Most churches and synagogues have appropriate decor for the religious significance of most occasions, but not when it comes to weddings. There may be a million candles, there will have to be more: there could be large amounts of greens and flowers, there will have to be more.

The flowers and decorations will not match the pre-selected colors and design of the wedding. With any luck, you will not have to worry about removing existing flowers and plants, but you certainly will have to deal with additional flowers and plants. I suspect that the favored plants also will be out of season for use of local flora. Rather, flowers ordered from half a globe away will be required to match the intended color scheme.

Most likely the enemy will not pick a color that cannot be matched in live flowers, but where they come from and how much the cost may be another issue. It could be orchids from Hawaii that are essential for the desired effect. It may be cheaper to pick up the guests and take them all to Hawaii rather then bring the plants to your home town; however, flowers are essential.

If you really did plan ahead, the religious leaders of your community have minimized the amount of flowers and decorations that they will allow in the sanctuary. If not—beware!

Unfortunately, it also will be almost impossible to utilize the same flowers and decorations that were used during the ceremony at the reception. Oh, you may get away with moving one or two floral arrangements, but otherwise additional materials will have to be provided at the reception, appropriate to the occasion.

A general rule of thumb for the bride's mother's attitude about flowers is that there can't be too many. She will prefer and demand the kind that are live, fresh and will wither within two days. They will have no other use and will not even last long enough to get them to the hospital to cheer up some depressed patient, should you think that nice. Besides viewing at the ceremony and reception, they will be good for only one thing—photographing, a subject we will deal with shortly.

What else? Well, you can almost do anything with decorations to alter the appearance of any room. If the reception hall looks like a ballroom you can change it to look like a circus. Or, if it looks like a circus, you can change it to look like a castle. The question is, why do you want to? Nevertheless, you can have lights, lasers, balloons, ribbons, streamers or create just about any mood you want, assuming, of course, you are willing to pay for it. If you want to look like you are outside, but you don't want to have the reception outside, no problem. If you are outside, but want the tent to look like a ballroom, still no problem. Get the idea?

Have the checkbook ready and remember that what goes up also must come down. Be sure to make arrangements to have the flowers and decorations removed and to leave the premises as you found them. It can be included in the rental agreement, for a price. Don't think you will get up the next day and clean it up yourself. We have plans for the next day.

CHECK LIST
Flowers and Decorations

❑ Get rule passed to prevent flowers and decorations in the church/synagogue sanctuary, or
❑ Use locally grown flowers
❑ Express your love of ferns (they are inexpensive)
❑ Call "rent a flower"
❑ Examine existing flowers in church/synagogue—unfortunately they will be unacceptable to the enemy
❑ Buy flowers and decorations for church/synagogue
❑ Buy flowers and decorations for reception
❑ Buy flowers and decorations for everything else
❑ Color coordinate all flowers and decorations
❑ Add more candles
❑ Change appearance of the room—no matter what it looks like
❑ Add more flowers
❑ Arrange for clean up—don't you do it
❑ Don't let your wife intimidate you

Photography and Videography

Wedding ceremonies rarely last longer than an hour and often much less then that. Receptions may last four or five hours and they also are over, and for that you are spending a small fortune, or perhaps a large one. It is very evanescent.

But fear not, you can suitably record the events so that you can savor the glorious day, moment by moment for eternity. Of course, to accomplish that you have to spend some more money. You have to engage a photographer.

I will admit there are a variety of ways to deal with the photography issue. Since we all consider ourselves semi-professional photographers, we should be able to do it ourselves. You did accumulate all that expensive photographic equipment through the years, didn't you? You could get it all out, read the directions carefully and become sufficiently acquainted with the techniques that you could get high quality images. But remember the instructions are written in Japanese and you don't read Japanese.

Besides, you will be too busy. But Cousin John won't be too busy; why don't you ask him to bring his camera and act as photographer? Well, it just won't work. Oh, plenty of guests will bring cameras and want to record the event. They will make a lot of flashes throughout the ceremony and reception but you won't get much in the way of quality. No, you will have to find a professional to do the job.

And, you better treat the search of a professional photographer the same way you did for the music and caterer. Investigate the quality of the photography, ask for and talk to references and discuss price very carefully.

You will need a variety of photographs. First, you will need an engagement picture. Then you will need a formal wedding picture. These will have to be portrait type photos and probably will require a studio sitting and a different photographer than the photos you want of the ceremony and reception.

The candid photos of the ceremony and reception do follow rather traditional poses, with group shots of the wedding party, certain scenes of the ceremony and lots of photos of guests, cake cuttings, bouquet throwing and so forth. Be sure to plan the individuals you want the photographer to include in the candid shots. After all, you certainly don't want to leave anyone out and thereby insult them. In fact, it is probably a good idea to make actual lists of these important friends and relatives to ensure they are included. Countless hours of discussion can be consumed by this project alone.

The photographs have to be professionally done, proofs provided, choices made and finally an album created to record the event. Did I say album? I should have said albums. The bride and groom certainly need one. But how about a smaller version for the parents of the bride, the parents of the groom, something for the grandparents, siblings, friends, relatives....get the picture? Maybe you think everyone should pay for their own albums? O.K., if you can pull it off, go ahead, but be prepared to provide your "loved ones" something.

So much for the still photography. You are not done yet. We have to talk about video. In the old days, there were movies. I have them from my wedding. Periodically we take them out, look at them (if we can find a projector that works), and remark about all the guests. I think you can figure out what has happened to most of them by now. In fact, we intend to have the movies converted to video tapes so that we can view them more easily.

Well, you don't have to worry about movies. You can go directly to video. Once again, you have some decisions. How many cameras do you want to use to record the event? Just like at a professional football game or other sporting event, the more cameras the better the coverage. Several cameras, recording from different angles and viewpoints will make for a better video. Do you want the entire ceremony and reception recorded? No problem, just need more film and editing. Do you want sound? No problem and no extra charge unless you want voice-over describing the event. How about titles? They really do make the video more enjoyable.

Since by now you are so deeply committed to the wedding process you are long past "the point of no return," you better go for the whole photography effort. It's all you have left to remember the day. All left, that is, besides the paid bills. You certainly won't have any money.

CHECK LIST
Photography and Videography

❏ Choose photographer
    Avoid amateur friend or relative
    Choose professional for:
        Engagement
        Formal portrait
        Candid's of ceremony and reception
❏ Ask for references
❏ Look at portfolio of previous work
❏ Choose proofs
❏ Choose albums for: Bride and groom, Parents, Grandparents, Others
❏ Choose videographer
    Avoid amateur friend or relative
    Choose professional
❏ Specify number of cameras
❏ Specify length of video
❏ Specify sound
❏ Specify titles
❏ Copies for: Bride and groom, Parents, Grandparents, Others
❏ Ask for references
❏ Look at sample videos of previous work
❏ Don't let your wife intimidate you

The Hairstylist

It doesn't matter whether your daughter has never been to a beauty salon in her life or whether she has hair so short that she could be a Marine, she will have to have her hair "done" on the day of the wedding. No big deal. You have invested so much already that you can easily afford this expense.

By the way, it's not just the bride. Don't forget the mother of the bride, the sisters of the bride, the grandmothers of the bride, and who knows who else. They will all need this service and it will be up to you to provide it.

There are two schools of thought on the best way to do this. The bride and everyone else could go to the hairstylist and have the work done in his or her shop. This may give the bride a few hours of peace in all the commotion. The other alternative is to have the hairstylist come to the bride and do the work in your home, or wherever the ceremony will take place.

I'm sure you understand that if this was done in the morning, there will still have to be touch ups done even up to the walk down the aisle. It will be much better to keep the hairstylist handy for these last minute fixes. By now you realize that this will cost extra, since it will require several hours. Of course, you probably will want to invite the hairstylist to the reception. After all, he or she is providing an invaluable service and the simple fee will not really be enough.

It is conceivable that since your family has been faithfully using the same hairstylist for many years, and he or she has become at least a confidant if not actually a member of the family, the stylist may donate his or her services as a gift. If that is the case, you better make sure the invitation to the reception is given and with thanks.

CHECK LIST
The Hairstylist

❑ Choose hairstylist
❑ Decide if the bride should go to the salon
❑ Decide regarding an all day engagement with the stylist available throughout
❑ Consider having your newly acquired grey hair tinted
❑ Don't let your wife intimidate you

Transportation

I don't know what type of business you are in, but I doubt many of you are in the transportation business—yet. Get ready, because you soon will become experts in transportation. Regardless of the size of the wedding, or the number of guests invited, some of them will almost certainly be from out of town. In some cases, this may be the majority of the guests.

How will they get from the airport to their lodgings? Don't tell me it's not your problem. It is. After all, you invited these people; if you don't believe that check out the invitation.

The answer to your problem is to determine the arrival times and the numbers of guests and either hire a bus, limo or taxi to pick them up. If there are enough of them, several may arrive close to the same time. If there are only a few, you won't be so lucky. Either way it probably will require several trips.

If you think you can get local friends or family to do the airport pick up, think again. You don't need any last minute conflicts or confusion. Your life will be difficult enough. Spend the money to maintain your own sanity.

Now that the out of town guests are here, you still have to worry about getting them where they have to be and on time. One alternative is to keep all the activities and functions within walking distance. If the hotel is situated very close to the site of the ceremony, the reception, the rehearsal dinner and your home, then you have it made. Unfortunately, that is not likely to happen and you will be faced with arranging for a variable number of people to be transported at varying times. If you have the opportunity to arrange any of the locations of these functions with transportation in mind, I think it is better to transport guests to and from the ceremony and let them walk home after the reception, since they probably will not all want to leave at the same time.

More than likely, you will have to transport everyone everywhere. You might as well arrange for appropriate transportation for the entire wedding weekend, or wedding week, whatever it turns out to be.

When you consider the types of transportation available, you probably will have to utilize different types for different functions. For example, a chartered bus would be quite suitable for everyone to get to the rehearsal dinner. But please don't use the same bus to get the bride to the ceremony. How about a limo or a horse and buggy for an unusual trip? Some people get very exotic about this and such modes of travel as a helicopter, sled or boat have been used. Please consider the difficulty the bride will have with the very large and cumbersome dress. She will need room, particularly to get to the ceremony and reception. Give her a break.

Transportation does not end with the reception. Your guests will have to get from place to place for their entire stay, including getting back to the airport so they can go home. This part of the transportation may be the best for you. It certainly pays to make sure you get them to the plane on time.

CHECK LIST
Transportation

❏   Choose transportation vendor
❏   Arrange transportation from:
      Airport to hotel
      Hotel to rehearsal dinner and return
      Hotel to church/synagogue
      Church/synagogue to reception
      Reception to hotel
      Hotel to airport
❏   Choose appropriate type of transportation for each occasion
      Limousine
      Bus
      Taxi
      Horse and carriage
      Helicopter
      Other
❏   Don't let your wife intimidate you

Security

We do need to discuss one arrangement that is well worth the expense. It will pay for you to consider appropriate security measures during the wedding events. Unfortunately, it's not like the old days. I suppose there are some communities where you can leave the front door of your home open, knowing that the house and contents will still be safe. But there aren't many of them and more than likely you will need security.

You should make arrangements for someone to be in your home while you and all of the family are out celebrating. Remember, the events surrounding the wedding will be well known to a variety of people. It doesn't take a genius to figure that the house will be empty when everyone is at the ceremony or reception. Make sure someone is home and visibly home. It wouldn't hurt if that someone was an off duty police officer.

It also will be comforting to your guests to know that security is available at the various functions. Even if the ceremony is at a church or synagogue, having another off duty police officer in the parking lot and around the premises will be important.

If the reception is at a hotel, in all likelihood there will be security already available. But it is a good idea to make sure and to insist that the hotel's security personnel is visible in and around the reception activities and checking on the vehicles of the guests.

If the hotel or reception hall does not provide this security, then it certainly pays for you to arrange it and some reception halls will insist that you make security available. They will charge you for it, but it is another item that is relatively inexpensive and worth the price.

CHECK LIST
Security

❑ Arrange security for:
Your home
Church/synagogue
Reception
❑ Let a thief steal your wife's credit cards. He won't spend as much
❑ Don't let your wife intimidate you

Gifts

I know what you are thinking, here comes the good part. Good for whom? Don't get too excited—it won't be for you.

In the average wedding situation, gifts go two ways—out and in. You will have to give a variety of gifts to a variety of individuals. The bride and groom will receive gifts from a variety of individuals. You will get nothing. Not much has changed, has it?

Who gets these gifts you give? It will seem like everyone. First of all, the maid of honor should get a gift, that will come from the bride. You know who that is; for gift giving purposes, you are the bride. The bridesmaids also will get gifts that traditionally include the jewelry they will wear at the ceremony. You also need to include a jewelry box, suitable for display that they can use to store the jewelry when they are not wearing the pearl necklace and diamond earrings that you give them. There also will be members of the house party that will need gifts; members of the house party are very important to the affair, but I am not quite sure exactly what their functions include. Don't worry about it, you need them and the enemy will find plenty for them to do. Just include them on your gift list.

Time for some good news: the best man and the groomsmen also will need gifts, but you don't have to worry about them. That is the responsibility of the groom or his family.

The groom also has to provide gifts for the clergypersons. These individuals usually do not charge a fee for their services but they do expect, and should receive, a monetary donation. If they are long-standing friends of yours, they may insist they do not want a gift. Even so, a donation to the church or synagogue, particularly directed to the clergyperson's discretionary fund, is always in order.

It is also nice to provide gifts to some or all of the guests at the wedding. The out of town visitors might appreciate a gift of some local importance that they can take home and enjoy as a remembrance. If you really get into the gift giving mood, try a copy of this book to all the male guests present. It certainly should demonstrate your friend-ship.

If you are going to buy gifts in bulk, make sure you buy plenty of them. You will find needs you never anticipated and precious little time to run out and pick something up at the last minute. Plan ahead.

Shortly after the engagement is announced, the future bride and groom will start receiving gifts and gifts will continue to arrive even after the wedding. It's one of the best times of their lives. They will enjoy it. You also will be interested in the process and you probably will want to inspect the gifts and compare the type and quality of the gift with the giver. Get ready for some surprises.

You may find some of the most expensive gifts coming from the most unlikely sources, and vice versa. Don't be surprised if there are many duplicate gifts. After all, how much variation can you expect? Don't be surprised if some of the gifts appear used (they may have been) or if some of the gifts look familiar. It won't be the first time someone has given a gift he or she has received from someone else and the someone else could have been you. It is difficult to remember who gave you what.

All in all, the gifts need to be recorded and acknowledged; that is the responsibility of the bride and groom. This is a very onerous task but one that should be done as quickly as possible. It is better to avoid a gift giver asking if the gift arrived because no thank you note was received.

Your daughter will want to "register" at several local and national stores so that potential gift givers can purchase gifts that are appropriate. Certainly the chosen pattern for china, crystal and flatware should be on record so that consistency can be maintained. This is the new couple's chance to acquire the necessities for beginning their life together, and if they don't get these items as gifts, someone close to you may have to provide them. Don't minimize this process.

Once again, if thank you notes are not promptly sent, the gift givers will blame you. It doesn't matter that the gifts were given to the bride and groom. You are the father of the bride and even if you didn't get the gift, you did raise your daughter. You obviously did a poor job since she can't even send a little note. The secret, of course, is to stay on top of the job and not let the note writing get out of hand.

CHECK LIST
Gifts

☐ Help buy (read that "pay for") gifts for:
    Maid of honor
    Bridesmaids
    Houseparty
    Out of town guests
    Others
    Someone you forgot
☐ Do not help to buy gifts for:
    Best man
    Groomsmen
    Clergy—but make sure the groom did it for the clergypersons
☐ Help choose gift registry for the guests' gift selections
☐ Don't be surprised about who gives what
☐ Remind bride and groom to send prompt thank you notes
☐ Remind them again
☐ Don't let your wife intimidate you

Out Of Town Guests

We have talked about these out of town guests before. We need to discuss them and their issues a bit further. Everyone who will make the trip for this wedding will be someone special to you. Were they to visit at any other time, you would spend considerable time with them, entertaining them, showing them the town and perhaps even having them stay with you, in your home. Now it's different. You certainly cannot treat the hoards of close friends and family that will descend on you the same way you would treat them individually. They don't expect it. Or at least, if they do, don't worry about it. You do, however, have to make arrangements for them and their comfort and entertainment while they are in town.

First, you need to find them a place to stay by choosing a local hotel or motel that will be appropriate. Consider the cost, but also consider the convenience to the activities, the ambiance of the hotel and the abilities of the guests to pay their hotel bill. You might want to review the section on transportation.

We have already decided that they probably will be included in the rehearsal dinner if they get into town the night before. If they will not be included, but will be in town, find something for them to do.

On the day of the wedding they will have to have breakfast. They can usually do that on their own, and if they had a really good time the night before, at the rehearsal dinner, they may even sleep through breakfast. But they won't sleep through lunch. What are you going to do about lunch? Perhaps an open house, sponsored and given by a friend? Better plan for something.

Of course, you shouldn't have much problem with dinner, if it is included as part of the wedding reception. The bottom line is regardless of when the ceremony and reception takes place, the meals the rest of the time have to be considered. That includes breakfast, or better, brunch the next day. If everyone is staying at the same place, you could have something there, at your home or someplace in between. If this is a sizable group you will have to start with more catering and other vendors and if you are not careful, it could turn into a mini-wedding.

Now, you can avoid all of this and let these people fend for themselves, but they will be in a strange city and many of them may be older individuals who find it difficult to get around. Don't worry, the enemy will take care of the details and all you will have to do is pay.

CHECK LIST
Out Of Town Guests

☐ Be hospitable
☐ Choose accommodations carefully
☐ Provide transportation for all activities
☐ Provide entertainment for:
    Rehearsal dinner
    Wedding day meals
    Day after wedding meals
    Free time activities
☐ Don't let out of town guests stay too long
☐ Remember out of town guests are like fish–they start to smell after three days
☐ Don't let your wife intimidate you

EMERGENCY SITUATIONS

There has never been a wedding, no matter how meticulously planned and executed, that didn't encounter some emergency situations. Yours will be no exception.

Emergencies will fall into two categories—minor and major. Don't worry about the minor emergencies. If the ice sculpture looks like it was carved by Godzilla, don't worry about it. If the addresses on the invitations look like they were written by a six-year-old with a crayon, don't worry about it.

There are a variety of major emergencies that you will have to deal with. First of all, sometime during the planning process, the bride will come home and announce the marriage is off. Here we have a real problem. I know you have already paid a king's ransom in deposits to every conceivable and some inconceivable vendors and you and the enemy have announced the impending wedding to everyone you know in the whole world. And here comes your baby, the light of your life, telling you she hates her fiance, his family, your wife and everyone else.

Considering the pressures on her, from all sources, about the planning of this event, it is not surprising. I suppose you wonder why it hasn't happened before.

Hope and pray that this is not serious and just the standard pre-wedding jitters. The jitters are a common problem. Everyone gets them but the pressure on the bride is tremendous. Take her aside, alone, and have a heart to heart talk with her. In fact, it probably will take several talks about the problem. So common is the problem that you can anticipate its development. Take some time to do preventive discussions with her periodically and perhaps you can avoid this emergency.

In most cases, it will pass.

The next emergency may be more difficult to deal with: one day the groom will announce that he wants to call the wedding off. Now you have a different problem. You still have a considerable financial investment in the impending wedding, but you do not have the same feelings for him as you do for your daughter.

In fact, if you happen to be in one of the situations where you actually dislike you future son-in-law, you may really have ambivalent feelings about this emergency. If he is really the "bum" you always thought, you may be willing to lose the money and encourage the cancellation of the wedding. On the other hand, it's possible that you like your future son-in-law, perhaps even more than your daughter, and you may have been counting on the wedding as a way to "get rid of her—legally." If that is the case, you better do something fast. Figure out what the problem is and take some corrective action. This may be your last chance.

Another major emergency may be beyond your control: true illness can actually strike anyone. If illness does occur to some key person in the wedding party, plans may have to be changed.

Your own illness probably would be the most important to you, you selfish person. But what about illness of the bride, the groom, the mother of the bride, the clergyperson, or someone in the wedding party? Books have been written and movies made about some of these unusual circumstances. The bride wearing a cast on her leg due to a skiing accident is one example. Well, the cast can be suitably covered with lace and it makes in interesting story. Your heart attack that lands you in the coronary intensive care unit three days before the wedding is another story. I really can't give you advice on how to handle illness like this. Substitutes can always be found, but there are times when plans may have to be changed, and I would suggest your clergypersons as a good resource to advise you or your family on these matters. They have had a lot of experience with illness. Use them.

We need to talk about weather emergencies. There is nothing like a good hurricane to mess up wedding plans, even if the ceremony and reception are to take place indoors. Just a plain heavy rain at the wrong time can ruin things. None of us can control the weather, but we can certainly pray for the best. Even if you are not a religious person, for all you have invested in this wedding, it wouldn't hurt to hedge your bet and pray a little.

There are other emergencies, perhaps not of the same significance as illness or hurricane, that can still cause you trouble.

We have discussed the predictable ratio of invitations sent to numbers of invitees accepting. Generally, there will be a considerable number of friends and family who will be unable to attend. Unless, that is, they all do want to attend. You may find yourself in the position that more people will be coming than you planned for or can afford. You now have a problem. If you sent the invitations out early enough, you will have time to make some additional accommodations, including finding a larger hall, ordering more food and spending considerably more money. At least you will have time to arrange bank financing.

If you were late with the invitations and still too many guests accept your invitation, you will have to scramble. The caterer will have some extra food but not enough for too many more eaters. If invited guests bring uninvited guests along you may really have a problem. It is inappropriate for anyone to arrive uninvited, but you know how some people are. If one of your friends has some company from out of town for the weekend, he may want to bring them along. He certainly should ask first, and then you will have the option of allowing the additional people to come along or refusing and risk losing the friend and his presence at the festivities. You will have to deal with this on a case by case or friend by friend basis.

You may be faced with the opposite problem. You may have sent out many invitations, expecting a large number of guests to participate, only to find out that for some reason or another very few people respond that they will attend. Meanwhile, you may have planned and paid for a much larger number. There is no question that it is easier to downsize the wedding then to increase the size. Reception halls can be screened to look smaller and caterers can be instructed to prepare for fewer guests. In most cases, if they are given enough advance notice they will understand your predicament. Do not call up the morning of the wedding and inform the caterer that only half the number of guests you "guaranteed" to be present will be present. You will be expected to pay for the previously agreed upon numbers, as the food has probably already been prepared, and it has certainly been purchased. The only good news about such a predicament is that you can and should request the extra food be delivered to you, for use at other times. You may have to buy a new freezer to accommodate it.

What do you intend to do when you discover that someone very important to you or your family was inadvertently left off the guest list? Your immediate reaction, if you discover this before the wedding, is to contact the person and blame the United States Postal Service for the loss of the invitation. That's an old story and everyone has used it before. I don't think it will do much. Rather, I believe it is best to come clean with the person, explain how crazy things have been with all these plans and apologize for the lateness of the invitation, but insist that it is your honest desire to have him join you at the wedding. If you sound (and are) sincere it will usually work.

What to do if you don't discover this until after the wedding? It is still best to contact the individuals and explain the error as best you can, apologizing profusely and hope they will understand. It would be nice to invite them and the bridal couple out to dinner, but I would not subject them to the entire video of the wedding. Your good friends should understand. Of course, if you forgot Aunt Sadie (which you may have done on purpose), you can and should expect your lumps.

Speaking of lumps, sometime or another during the wedding planning process, there may be actual fighting that occurs. I mean actual physical confrontation. I can't predict who the antagonists will be. Almost any combination is possible, depending on the circumstances and particular issues involved. Just be sure you are not one of them. You need to be ready to step in and stop all verbal and physical violence. For, if not you....then who?

These are only a few of the possible emergency situations that can occur. You will find you own. It is important to remember that you need to stay flexible, think quickly and be honest. Such an attitude probably will serve you best during these trying times.

CHECK LIST
Emergency Situations

☐ Expect emergencies
☐ Anticipate emergencies and develop responses
☐ Show concern, but remember they will pass
☐ Have physician stand by
☐ Don't call off the wedding due to the bride's anxiety
☐ Don't call off the wedding due to the groom's anxiety
☐ Prepare for weather impact
☐ Monitor RSVP's. Hope you don't get too many yeses
☐ Check list to make sure you didn't forget someone
☐ Make contingency plans if too many or too few RSVP's are returned
☐ Don't panic
☐ Don't let your wife intimidate you

FINAL WORDS

At times I have given you advice and you know from your own experiences what to do with most advice. At times I have suggested that you take the easy way out, and go along with the enemy, especially when something is inevitable.

I hope the information contained herein helps you. In retrospect, I can report to you that it did not help me at all. In some cases, I discovered the facts too late. In others, I was victimized just as you will be.

Please remember a few final words: Remember Murphy's Law: "If something can go wrong it will!" It is a little known fact, but Murphy discovered this law while he was planning his own daughter's wedding.

Write all checks and pay all bills with a smile. It won't save you any money but it will minimize the gloating that the vendors will want to do.

Finally, stay calm! At least that will separate you from the rest of the wedding party

Post Script

I hope you have enjoyed the material contained in this manual. I would be remiss and also crazy if I did not include a disclaimer that all of this was written tongue-in-cheek. Of course, all these people are not the enemy. Of course, we appreciate the great job they did with our weddings. And of course, we understand the stress everyone went through with all the planning. WE DO APPRECIATE IT!

(There, dear, I hope that makes you happy!)